IMAGES
of America

WINSTON-SALEM'S AFRICAN AMERICAN LEGACY

D1528897

The limited opportunities that both middle and low income African Americans experienced from racial discrimination and segregation bonded them together regardless of social and economic status. African Americans organized through social organizations to take civic action and provide community service advancement of African Americans in Winston-Salem. Pictured in this 1965 photograph are members of the Alpha Phi Alpha fraternity and their wives, who were widely involved in serving the African American community. The Alpha brothers pictured are, from left to right, (first row) R. Ogden; (second row) P. Simmons; (third row) unidentified, C. Martin, R. Frazier, W. McCloud, J. Greenwood, G. Newell, T. Hooper, J. Jones, H. Ward, C.J. Sawyer, G. Vaughn, W. Pitts, and L. Hall. (Courtesy of Dr. Willard McCloud.)

ON THE COVER: Taken in 1954 by well-known photographer Frank Jones, this photograph shows the band of the Atkins High School in the Winston-Salem Christmas parade marching down North Liberty Street. Atkins High School, listed in the National Register of Historic Places, was dedicated on April 2, 1931, as a facility for African American children. The school is named for Dr. Simon Green Atkins, the founder of Winston-Salem State University. (Courtesy of FCPL.)

IMAGES
of America

WINSTON-SALEM'S
AFRICAN AMERICAN
LEGACY

Cheryl Streeter Harry

Published by Arcadia Publishing
Charleston, South Carolina

Printed in the United States of America

Library of Congress Control Number: 2012940623

For all general information, please contact Arcadia Publishing:
Telephone 843-853-2070
Fax 843-853-0044
E-mail sales@arcadiapublishing.com
For customer service and orders:
Toll-Free 1-888-313-2665

Visit us on the Internet at www.arcadiapublishing.com

*To my husband, Miles, my sons Micah and Marcus, and my
mothers, Clydia Streeter Mitchell and Anne Streeter Harding,
and to the enslaved Africans of Salem and Winston.*

CONTENTS

FOREWORD

History is merely an autobiography of memories, and a shared expression of who we are.

History is the witness that testifies to the passing of time; it illumines reality, vitalizes memory, provides in daily life and brings us tidings of antiquity.

—Cicero, *Pro Publio Sestio.*

This book of chronicled experiences gives shape and definition to the City of Winston-Salem, North Carolina. This book illuminates historical landmarks, communities, events, and the people who make this community a portrait of beauty.

As one peruses this book, it is important to feel the spirit for which it was arranged. The spirit of this book is marked by the faith of people to succeed and achieve in the areas of the arts, athletics, education, business, medicine, music, manufacturing, spirituality, economics, and political and civic leadership.

This book of memoirs offers researched documentation of linear events that raise consciousness and awareness to how far we as a community have come. This historical reflection is paramount for interpreting the development of a past community, and it carries the intention to inspire the present community. The present community must be like the African Sankofa bird that has the ability to fly forward while looking backward. This will inevitably make Winston-Salem a better place to live.

Although the primary focus of this book is the African American community, the knowledge, wisdom, and information gained from this pictorial collage are significant to any community that is serious about valuing the journey and the story of people. It is a story that must be told and shared with generations to come. Therefore, these photographs capture yesteryear in a way that makes the obvious come alive—a tremendous price has already been paid, and a new bill is in the mailbox.

Each photograph has been carefully selected and placed upon these pages. Pay close attention to the mood of the day, the reflection within the eyes, and the facial expressions that alone can write chapters from now to eternity. These photographs carry the essence of showered optimism with a misty spray of hope that tomorrow will always be a better photograph.

—Dr. Sir Walter Mack Jr.
Pastor and Teacher
Union Baptist Church, Winston-Salem

ACKNOWLEDGMENTS

This publication would not have been possible without the support of many people. Deepest gratitude is due to my colleagues Dr. Michael and Martha Hartley for their efforts to shine the light on African American history in Winston-Salem and for their encouragement to take on this project, and to Kym Maddocks and Brenda Pledger, my dear associates who listened and provided research assistance. Special thanks to Dr. Maya Angelou, Bettie Clay, Old Salem Museums & Gardens and MESDA, local archivists and historians Billy Rich, Lester Davis, Tom Flynn, Rosa Wilson, Weldon Hay, Commander Kim Caesar, Ralph Meadows, and Fam Brownlee. Thanks to scholars and authors Dr. Lenwood Davis, Dr. William Rice, and Dr. James McLaughlin for their prior work that provided a foundation for this present work. To my friends Patricia Ford, Monica Mack Covington, Mütter Evans, Sherri Grant, and Denise Meeks-Blount, and my guardians Delores Scales and Sam and Inez Gray, for their support over the years. Most special thanks to my husband, who unwittingly became coauthor and photographer. I offer my sincere appreciation to all those people who willingly opened their doors to me to share their memories, without which this book would not have possible. I also wish to thank my editor, Katie McAlpin, and the wonderful staff at Arcadia Publishing.

The images in this volume appear courtesy of the Society for the Study of Afro-American History (SSAH), Winston-Salem State University Archives-C.G. O'Kelly Library (WSSU-CGOL), Forsyth County Public Library Photograph Collection (FCPL), Wachovia Historical Society (WHS), Old Salem Museums & Gardens (OSMG), and *The Winston-Salem Chronicle* (*The Chronicle*).

INTRODUCTION

Out of the huts of history's shame
I rise
Up from a past that's rooted in pain
I rise
I'm a black ocean, leaping and wide,
Welling and swelling I bear in the tide.
Leaving behind nights of terror and fear
I rise
Into a daybreak that's wondrously clear
I rise
Bringing the gifts that my ancestors gave,
I am the dream and the hope of the slave.
I rise
I rise
I rise.

—Maya Angelou, *Still I Rise*

A wealth of historical information and artifacts were recovered during the restoration of the African Moravian churches and graveyards in Old Salem during the 1990s. From the meticulously kept records of the Moravian Church, we know in detail about the work and religious life of Africans in Salem. One can envision Africans working as slaves in Wachovia (now Forsyth and Stokes Counties); or visualize Nancy, who was born in West Africa around 1749, cooking at the Salem Tavern during George Washington's visit; or the enslaved John Emmanuel, who spoke German better than English, interpreting for the Moravians as their English speaking patrons entered the tavern. Then there's Jupiter, the son of an African king, enslaved in the settlement of Hope just six miles from Salem. What did enslaved Africans do when work was over and they were alone to themselves in the Negro Quarter, on the Schumann Plantation, and other dwellings of privacy? What songs did they sing, what art did they create, what did they write, and what were their socio-cultural concerns? To date, we do not have any early records or photographs that reflect their way of life. As a community historian, this pictorial is my earnest attempt to record the social and cultural engagement of African Americans in Winston-Salem from 1800 to 1998. *Winston-Salem's African American Legacy* reflects our cultural property—our music, our art, our institutions, and our theology. It is a relational book full of images that will trigger poignant memories of a time gone by and provide inspiration for the future. This book is a testament to the contributions and vitality of the people and organizations that have determined the cultural and social pursuits of Winston-Salem. This publication is only the tip of the iceberg. There are so many more books to be written about Winston-Salem's African American history. Perhaps this publication will ignite a wildfire of historical vigilantes in our community dedicated to the preservation of African American history.

One

KEEPERS OF THE CULTURE

In 1928, the Twin City Glee Club, an all male African American choral ensemble organized by Dr. A.L. Cromwell, presented a concert by ex-slaves in Winston-Salem's newly opened Carolina Theatre. Even though African Americans had to sit in the balcony while whites watched from the lower level, Dr. Cromwell felt it was important to have the voices of freedmen resounding in this segregated venue. Since slavery and up to this now supposedly post-racial age, many groups and individuals have been committed to making sure that the experiences of African Americans are kept alive and passed on to future generations. In West Africa it is the griot that is responsible for keeping an oral history. A griot can be a storyteller, dancer, musician, genealogist, historian, spokesman, or a diplomat. In Winston-Salem, it is no different. The Twin City's storytellers, dancers, writers, historians, politicians, and leaders pass on the history through performances, plays, forums, festivals, and special programs. In 1977, Rachel Jackson and the friends of the East Winston Library presented Winston-Salem's first Kwanzaa event. Shirley Holloway, known as the barefoot storyteller, was a part of this celebration of African American culture and history. Historical preservation efforts are led by advocates such as Rudolph Boone, Luci Vaughn, Lee Faye Mack, and Fleming El-Amin; journalists and writers such as Joe Watson, Layla Farmer, and Kevin Walker; performance artists such as playwright Nathan Ross Freeman, Sharon Frazier, and Horace Fulton; and actress and acclaimed choreographer Mabel Robinson. Dr. Carter G. Woodson, the founder of the Black History Month celebration, which began in 1926, is quoted as saying, "if a race has no history, if it has no worthwhile tradition, it becomes a negligible factor in the thought of the world, and it stands in danger of being exterminated."

In 1982, global renaissance woman Dr. Maya Angelou settled in Winston-Salem. This world renowned poet, educator, historian, best-selling author, actress, playwright, civil rights activist, producer, and director swiftly became a part of the cultural landscape, lending her name and support to many causes in the city, including the National Black Theatre Festival, the Amani Foundation, the Juneteenth Celebration, conversations at churches and forums, readings and book signings, and many more events. Dr. Angelou collaborated with three leading organizations in the city to address health disparities, all of which have named centers in her honor, including The Maya Angelou Center for Health Equity Wake Forest University Baptist Medical Center, The Maya Angelou National Institute for the Improvement of Child and Family Education at Winston-Salem State University, and the Maya Angelou Center for Women's Health and Wellness at Forsyth Medical Center. Dr. Angelou was appointed the First Reynolds Professor of American Studies at Wake Forest University, a lifetime appointment since 1981. (Courtesy of Dr. Maya Angelou; photograph by Dwight Carter.)

Many of the strides made by African Americans and the collection of black history can be attributed to Dr. Virginia Newell's efforts. Dr. Newell's zeal for achievement and progress among African Americans has made her a trailblazer in the city. She has held public office, worked as a mathematics professor, and served on numerous boards. In 1971, she started and coauthored the first book on black mathematicians. (Courtesy of *The Chronicle*.)

Genealogist and historian Mel White spearheaded the revival of the oldest African American churches in North Carolina at Old Salem. The 1823 African Moravian Log Church was reconstructed and the St. Philips Moravian Church, which dates to 1861, was restored. He organized the exhibit Across the Creek: The Story of Happy Hill from 1816 to 1952, which documented the history of African Americans in the community of Happy Hill. (Courtesy of White Collection.)

Dr. Vivian H. Burke began public service in 1977, rising to Winston-Salem's mayor pro-tempore. She has worked to raise social and cultural consciousness throughout the city. A former educator, building strong black families and communities is her passion. She has a long history of recognizing organizations and individuals for their efforts to improve the quality of life in Winston-Salem. (Courtesy of the City of Winston-Salem.)

Larry Womble, a former high school principal, city councilman, and state legislator, is a driving force in the political and social arena. Since the early 1970s, he has worked to create awareness of African American contributions to our society and address culturally sensitive issues relevant to the well being of the black community. From proclamations to reparations, he has been at the forefront of history-making decisions. (Courtesy of *The Chronicle*.)

The Winston-Salem Chronicle was established by Ernie Pitt in 1974. The Chronicle was just the second African American newspaper in the city. The first was The People's Voice, founded by Carl Russell, former city alderman and founder of Russell Funeral Home. It is through the legacy of Carl Russell that Pitt says The Chronicle was launched. In the early days, Ernie could be seen personally distributing his papers to convenience stores and other businesses throughout the community. At that time, he was practically a one-man shop. At right, Ernie is with his wife, Elaine Pitt, in the production room of The Chronicle at the Patterson Avenue location. Both he and Elaine have led the paper in its growth. The Chronicle is Winston-Salem's longest running and most well-respected community newspaper. (Courtesy of The Chronicle.)

Ernie Pitt, founder of *The Chronicle*, hangs the sign at 2408 North Patterson Avenue, the newspaper's first location. Below, Ernie (second from left) supervises the circulation auditing of *The Chronicle* in 1978. This event marks the first time an African American newspaper in the state became a member of the prestigious ABC audit organization. *The Chronicle* has won numerous awards and is highly respected among its peer organizations. *The Chronicle* is more than a weekly newspaper in the city. It is a mirror that enables the community to see itself and reflect on its gains and its pains. *The Chronicle* has been vigilant in its reporting of the African American story. (Courtesy of *The Chronicle*.)

Annette Scippio wrote *Beyond These Walls*, documenting the Black church in Winston-Salem. She edited "African American Women 1900–1980" and "African American Neighborhoods to 1970," historical calendars for the Society for the Study of Afro American History. At the Delta Arts Center she established an exhibit of Thomas Day furniture at the state Museum of History and coordinated the installation of the Biggers Murals at Winston-Salem State University. (Courtesy of *The Chronicle*.)

Flonnie Anderson is credited with organizing the first black community theater in the South during the 1950s. She became the first black actress and director with the Little Theatre of Winston-Salem. In 1981, she organized the Flonnie Anderson Theatrical Association to provide a forum for regional actors to express themselves creatively and to provide cultural theater experiences to educate the community about African American history. (Courtesy of the Anderson family.)

The North Carolina Black Repertory Company was founded in 1979 by Larry Leon Hamlin. It is the first professional black theater company in North Carolina. The company is universally recognized for its artistic and administrative achievements and its international outreach program, The National Black Theatre Festival. Larry founded the Theatre Festival in 1989, which brings more than 65,000 people to Winston-Salem. Pictured below is the 1980s board of directors for the company. Pictured are, from left to right, (first row) Luellen Curry, Sylvia Sprinkle-Hamlin, Elwanda Ingram, Joyce Elam, and Annie Alexander; (second row) Harvey Kennedy, Wil Jenkins, Richard Ackerman, Irvin Hodge, Warren Leggett, and Harold Kennedy III. (Courtesy of *The Chronicle*.)

Pictured here are two of the company's earlier productions. Above is the cast of *Day of Absence*, a play that was performed on several occasions. The play is a satire about an imaginary southern town where all the black people have suddenly disappeared. The North Carolina Black Repertory Company presents several productions annually, two of which are the Martin Luther King Jr. Birthday Celebration and *Black Nativity* written by Langston Hughes. The company generally features members of its ensemble with frequent celebrity guest actors. They work with other theater companies from around the country. Pictured below is the cast from *Celebrations: A Musical Review*, written by Larry Leon Hamlin. Pictured are, from left to right, Michael Wright, Carlotta Samuels-Fleming, Chris Murrell, and Latonya Black. (Courtesy of *The Chronicle*.)

In 1988, Delores "D" Smith-Wylie became president and chief executive officer of the Winston-Salem Urban League. During her tenure, the city was facing racial tension, heightened crime, and social inequalities. She focused the Urban League's advocacy strategies toward success and self-sufficiency and initiated "Bridging the Gaps in Race Relations," a training program that creates a community that values the diversity of all people and cultures. (Courtesy of the Urban League.)

Linda Sutton has been actively preserving the hard-fought legacy of the African American right to vote since the early 1970s, starting out as a union organizer and special voter registration commissioner. She has served the city for many causes and in many organizations, such as the North Carolina Election Laws Review Commission, the A. Philip Randolph Institute, the Goler Community Development Corporation, and Democracy North Carolina. (Courtesy of the Sutton family.)

Hashim Saleh's mission is to educate, inspire, and uplift his community through cultural dance, music, and theater. Since 1976, Saleh has led Winston-Salem in the advancement of African culture and music. He is the director and a founding musician of the Otesha Creative Arts Ensemble. He has worked as a music accompanist for the North Carolina Black Repertory Company and several universities and colleges. (Courtesy of the Saleh family.)

The Healing Force was founded in 1975 by the husband and wife team of Joseph and Gail Anderson and includes their daughter, Sonji, and son, Karim. The group brings richness to the city through their African storytelling and music. They have performed at many community events and the National Storytelling Festival, pictured here. Their performances unite all ethnic groups through the "rhythm of the drum." (Courtesy The Healing Force.)

Amatullah Saleem founded Otesha Creative Arts Ensemble, the oldest professional African American dance company in North Carolina, with cofounders Ron Dutch and Gilbert Young. Many youths from low-income communities experienced African American culture through her efforts. Amatullah, who trained and performed with legendary artist Katherine Dunham, is also a storyteller. Her stories speak about the migration to the north by black Americans fleeing racism and segregation. (Courtesy of Triad Cultural Arts.)

Annie Hamlin Johnson, also called "Mama Marvtastic," is the queen of community theater. Her son, Larry Hamlin, is the founder of the National Black Theatre Festival and he coined the word "marvtastic" during an early festival. A marvelous and fantastic actress and storyteller, she takes her performances into schools, churches, and senior and community centers. Her stories portray African American life during slavery and reconstruction. (Courtesy of the Johnson family.)

Renee J. Andrews has worked over 30 years for the Forsyth County Public Library in Children's Services. In addition to sharing stories with books, Andrews also shares the gift of the oral tradition of storytelling. As a professional storyteller, she is a member of the National and North Carolina Association of Black Storytellers. She has volunteered with numerous cultural groups throughout the city. (Courtesy of the Andrews family.)

Pat Mardia Stepney is a storyteller and former librarian who worked in children's outreach. Called Mardia-Tale Waver, she is known for weaving folkloric tales and keeping the rich heritage of storytelling alive. She is the founder of the North Carolina Association of Black Storytellers and also the celebrity storyteller for the National Black Theatre Festival. She was involved in the early Kwanzaa and Juneteenth events. (Courtesy of the Stepney family.)

A concerted effort to teach children and families about African American history and culture was made when the Kemet School of Knowledge was founded in 1989 at Emmanuel Baptist Church by Dr. Alton Pollard, Dr. John Mendez, and Sharon Anderson. The school has developed into an annual summer camp. Pictured are, from left to right, Sharon Anderson, Betty Brayboy, Dr. John Mendez, Dr. Felecia Piggott-Long, Cynthia Williams, and Qwame Nyere. (Courtesy of the Piggott-Long Collection.)

Armenta Adams Hummings is a renowned concert pianist and a former associate professor of music at the Eastman School of Music. In 1993, she founded the Gateways Music Festival in Winston-Salem and served as the artistic director. Gateways is a national event to increase the visibility and viability of African American classical musicians. Armenta is a community activist with a heart for the well being of people. (Courtesy of Ralph Meadows.)

In 1950, WAAA became the first African American programmed radio station in North Carolina. The station was located on the corner of Liberty and Third Streets, in the heart of downtown's black business district. The announcers became household names and included Larry Williams, Fred "Steady Eddie" Allen, Robert "Bobcat" Roundtree, and Oscar "Daddy-Oh" Alexander, whose legendary *Daddy-Oh on the Patio* show aired from Ray's Roadside Drive-In on Highway 311. In 1979, Mütter Evans became the youngest African American and the second African American woman to own a radio station by purchasing the station at 26 years of age. Evans is pictured above in front of the station at its Indiana Avenue location. The station changed ownership in 2006. Pictured below is Larry Williams (left) with owner and general manager Mütter Evans. He signed the station on the air October 29, 1950. (Courtesy of the Evans Collection.)

WAAA provided broadcast jobs for many African Americans who may not have had an opportunity to work in the field. Evans, along with various program directors, trained and fine-tuned many announcers who would go on to work throughout the industry. Pictured above are some of the staff in 1980, from left to right, (seated) Beverly McFadden, Doris "T" Walker, Mütter Evans, Sondra Williams, and Elaine Gray; (standing) Cloys Cecil, Al Martin, Roderick Howard, Eric Moore, William McClain, Valerie Gantt, Emeruwa Rose, Charles Bohannon, Fred Graham, and State Alexander. Pictured below are several members of the programming staff a decade later, from left to right, Mike Foxx, Renee Vaughn, Mark Raymond, and Brian Monds. (Courtesy of the Evans Collection.)

WAAA was a community station that featured a live weekly public affairs program called *The Talk About Town*. This talk show featured local and national guests who discussed matters that particularly informed and educated the community about local, regional, and national issues. The station also featured interactive promotions including various listener contests to keep them engaged and loyal, annual beach trips, and educational and entertainment outings. Above, a winner claims her prize from music director Tina Carson (right) and on-air personality Keith Cee. Pictured below is Gerald Alston, former lead singer with The Manhattans, with a listener at a station-sponsored event at the Black Velvet Lounge. (Courtesy of the Evans Collection.)

Let's Talk Sports was a favorite live call-in show with guests on Monday nights and was an expansion of "980 Triple A's" sports coverage from high school to professional. Here, WAAA Sports Director Robert Eller (front) and special guest, the legendary coach and athletic director Clarence "Big House" Gaines field questions about Winston-Salem State University and sports in general. (Courtesy of the Evans Collection.)

In January 1981, Mütter Evans, owner and general manager of WAAA, started the Noon Hour Commemoration of Dr. Martin Luther King Jr.'s birthday five years before it became a legal national holiday. Initially, the program was held outside, but moved to the Benton Convention Center in 1987. Pictured above are, from left to right, NAACP president Walter Marshall, mistress of ceremonies Mütter Evans, and keynote speaker Dr. Ernie Wade. Thousands attend this program annually. (Courtesy of the Evans Collection.)

The Winston-Salem/Forsyth County Emancipation Association has been celebrating the signing of the Emancipation Proclamation since 1880 with programs and awards. From left to right are (first row) Evelena Clayborn, Alice Allen, Martha Jones, Josephine Jones, Betty Meadows, and Miller Allen; (second row) Joycelyn Johnson, Larn Dillard, and Dr. Manderline Scales; (third row) Judge Roland Hayes, Barbara Hayes, and Levitha Mack. Not pictured are S. Armstrong, A. Barber, J. Dowell, H. Kennedy, H. Kennedy, W. Long, R. Long, and R. Boone. (Courtesy of the Emancipation Association.)

The Society for the Study of Afro-American History was founded in 1938 and has published numerous historical documents on African Americans in Winston-Salem/Forsyth County. From left to right are (first row) Thelma Hines, Cheryl Bradshaw, Rev. Henry Lewis, Ella Whitworth, and Gloria Diggs-Banks, (second row) Sadie Daniels, Virginia Newell, Frankie Powell, unidentified, Marie Williamson, and Joan Cardwell, (third row) Donald McThompson, Lenwood Davis, William Rice, Harold Kennedy Jr., James McLaughlin, and Mel White. (Courtesy of SSAH.)

Ed and Miriam McCarter started selling products out of their home and in 1983 they opened the Special Occasions Bookstore. It was one of the largest black owned bookstores between Atlanta and Washington, DC. Special Occasions provided Afrocentric products, which included books, church supplies, Greek paraphernalia, and other gift items. Special Occasions relocated from Jetway Shopping Center to Martin Luther King Drive and remained open until 2011. (Courtesy of *The Chronicle*.)

Michael and Dana Suggs have been a vital part of the cultural community. Both had successful careers in corporate America and worked closely with African American organizations on a national, state, and local level. Dana designed a unique line of Kwanzaa holiday ornaments and accessories that were sold in major chain stores. The Suggs now own Body and Soul, an Afrocentric cultural gift store and boutique. (Courtesy of Triad Cultural Arts.)

Two

COLLECTIVE
EMPOWERMENT

African American social organizations have a long history of community engagement in Winston-Salem. They have unapologetically used their collective power to mobilize and support education, economic development, involvement in the political process, and leadership for youth. In 1918, women from churches and clubs organized the Phyllis Wheatley Home in response to segregated boarding houses. "The Answer to Prayers of 23 Twin City Negro Women" was the newspaper headline on January 2, 1927. The home not only provided lodging for women who came to Winston-Salem to work in the factories, but offered educational classes in the day and evening for men, women, boys, and girls by certified instructors. Today, Twin City men and women are still leading community-based initiatives to improve the quality of life. Fraternities and sororities have taken the lead in building programs to mentor males, provide etiquette training, and help fund college education through scholarship programs along with other social and service organizations such as The National Council of Negro Women, The Salvation Army, and the YWCA. Community Development Corporations (CDC) began to emerge to revitalize low and moderate-income African American neighborhoods, such as the East Winston CDC, Liberty CDC, S.G. Atkins CDC, and church led CDCs such as the Goler CDC by Goler AME Zion Church and Union CDC of Union Baptist Church. The flagship organizations, NAACP, YMCA, and the Urban League, are still working to level the playing field for African American youth and safeguard gains made during the Civil Rights Movement. In response to 21st century challenges, new initiatives have emerged in health care programs to close the gap in disparate treatment of African Americans. Winston-Salem State University's (WSSU) School of Health Sciences received $300,000 to provide a mobile health clinic for the community. The clinic provides health screenings free of charge and is used by churches and at all types of community events. "For the good of the race" is the unspoken mantra of African American service organizations.

According to an undated newspaper article, the "colored branch of the YMCA," formerly known as the Patterson Avenue YMCA and now known as the Winston Lake Family YMCA, has been in existence since 1911. The first known meeting location of this YMCA was in the Old Depot Street School. Depot Street is now Patterson Avenue and the YMCA met in the school until it burned in 1926. In the 1920s, community leaders both black and white saw the need for a permanent "Negro branch" building and their first goal was to acquire property. The leading black men favored the Old Depot Street Site, and in June 1927, they staged the first major all black money raising drive held in the state of North Carolina and possibly the entire South. Their goal of $25,000 was big money and they went after it "with a whoop and hollar." This c. 1940 photograph is of the nutrition class at the YMCA's Patterson Avenue location. (Courtesy of SSAH.)

In 1985, Richard Glover (left), the executive director of the Patterson Avenue YMCA, led the move to its present location on Waterworks Road. It was renamed Winston Lake Family YMCA. The YMCA was and continues to be a full service family YMCA. The YMCA's history thereafter is synonymous with one man, Mo Lucas, who brought the famed Youth Incentive Programs, now known as the YMCA Art programs, to the YMCA. These programs included but are not limited to the Boss Drummer, the Kadets, the majorettes, and more. Mo Lucas is also credited with bringing the Black Achievers Program to the YMCA and today it is renowned as one of the leading Black Achievers programs in the nation. Mo Lucas is pictured below. (Above, courtesy of *The Chronicle*; below, courtesy of Triad Cultural Arts.)

The Kate B. Reynolds Hospital opened in 1938 with 100 beds. On May 15, 1938, a citywide Negro Appreciation Service was held at the Bowman Gray Memorial Stadium to honor the hospital's donors and the city of Winston-Salem. The choir was comprised of 1,000 black voices anchored by the Winston-Salem Teacher's College 500 voice student chorus (now Winston-Salem State University). Often referred to as "Katie B," the hospital provided care for 32 years until Reynolds Memorial and Reynolds Health Center replaced it in 1970. F.W. Dulin, one of the hospital's administrators, and Mrs. G.J. Andrews, who was director of nursing, are pictured at left in 1969. Below are students in the nursing school in 1948. (Left, courtesy of the Ford Collection; below, courtesy of SSAH.)

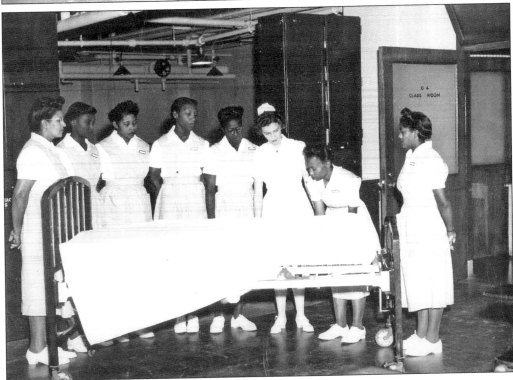

gro Leader J. T. McMillan Is Volatile and Involved

By Luix Overbea
Staff Reporter

1 T. McMillan is many things to many people.
ngregation of St. James AME Church at
atterson Avenue, where he has his office—he
door at the parsonage—he is the Rev. Mr.
pastor of their church and a potential bishop
frican Methodist Episcopal Church.

rent-Teacher Association leaders of the Twin
Council, he is a vocal president who some-
es statements on issues before the association
sed them.

bers of the new Interdenominational Minis-
ance, he is a volatile spokesman who sees its
preachers as men seeking fellowship and so-
their own particular problems, not as segre-
sters.

ple involved with the Experiment in Self-Re-
is agitator, friend or protector.

s wife, his son and two daughters, he is a
1.

Head of NAACP

Winston-Salem Branch of the National Asso-
the Advancement of Colored People, he is
lent.

o the visitor to his office, he is a busy man
ningly endless stream of telephone calls about
'A, funerals, the NAACP and people. He talks
rs while tackling other tasks.

n-Salem still needs the NAACP, McMillan said
view between phone calls. An atmosphere of
lf satisfaction" for Negroes and an attitude of
nong whites are retarding progress in race
1 the city, he said.

Staff Photo by Larry Martin
The Rev. J. T. McMillan — always at work.

The basic problems facing Negroes today, he
are:

—Labor's need to organize. "More unions are ne
here," he said. "There is a strong need for the or
ization of domestics. Negro leadership could streng
the community by helping people working as maids
cooks to organize."

—Housing and urban redevelopment. "Poor hou
is next to welfare as the greatest problem in the c

—And welfare. "There is nothing so ridiculou
the attitudes represented in welfare.

"On one hand there are youthful, healthy pe
who would rather receive welfare than work. On
other hand there are overpowering, self - determi
and dominating agencies which allow little freedor
welfare recipients."

Membership in Alliance

McMillan also talked about his membership in
Interdenominational Ministers Alliance, a reactiv
Negro group.

"This does not mean I am for segregation,"
said. "For more than two years, I have listene
these ministers express their concern for prob
unique to the Negro minister and for problems to w
the ultraconservative Forsyth Ministers Fellowshi
not willing to address itself.

"I agree with the sentiments of Rev. Pitts (D
Mack Pitts, pastor of Shiloh Baptist Church), 'He
an organization where we can take off our shoes
enjoy fellowship, where there are no big "I's" and l
"you's.'"

He added that he intends to continue to be ac
in the ministers fellowship. "I expect not only to
ticipate but plan to encourage more of our minis
to greater participation," he said.

In 1967, Rev. J.T. McMillan was elected as president of the Winston-Salem branch of the NAACP, replacing Carl Montgomery, a three-term president. In an interview with *The Journal* in 1967, McMillan described the basic problems facing African Americans as the need for cooks and maids to organize, substandard housing, and the welfare program. Not so much the recipients taking advantage of the program but the controlling agencies that allow little freedom to welfare recipients. McMillan's tenure included an emphasis on education, as McMillan was chairman of the Negro Twin City PTA Council, police brutality, voter education programs, and membership. McMillan went on to become one of the most revered NAACP leaders. Some of McMillan's officers were Dr. Jerry Drayton, Carl Russell, Rev. Warnie Hay, Dr. Kelly Goodwin, Jack Atkins, Dr. P.L. Brandon, C.C. Ross, Sarah Marsh, and Dr. David Hedgley. (Courtesy of the *Winston-Salem Journal*.)

Patrick Hairston served as president of the NAACP from 1976 to 1985. He opened the NAACP's first permanently staffed office. He worked to end segregated public facilities and received numerous awards for his vital role in membership and voter registration drives. He is remembered for his continuous fight in the struggle against injustices. He is pictured above (right forefront) with former national NAACP president Benjamin Hooks (left forefront). (Courtesy of the Hairston family.)

Walter Marshall served as president of the NAACP from 1986 into the 1990s. Marshall was the leading player in the settlement of the case that resulted in the desegregation of the Winston-Salem/ Forsyth County Schools. He also obtained victory in cases that resulted in election redistricting for the Forsyth County Boards of Education and County Commissioners. He is pictured here (left) with Jessie Jackson. (Courtesy of the Marshall family.)

The Winston-Salem Urban League was founded in 1947 through the efforts of James G. Hanes, who was concerned about negative race relations. Originally named the Community Relations Project, the organization became the Winston-Salem Urban League in 1953 and was chartered as an affiliate of the National Urban League in 1955. The Urban League Guild was created and chartered in 1955. Pictured above, from left to right, are John Jacob, former national president of the Urban League, and Irene Hairston and Marshall Bass, former chairs of the league's board. Pictured below is Urban League employee Cleopatra Solomon presenting Jacob with an award. (Above, courtesy of the Winston-Salem Urban League; below, courtesy of *The Chronicle*.)

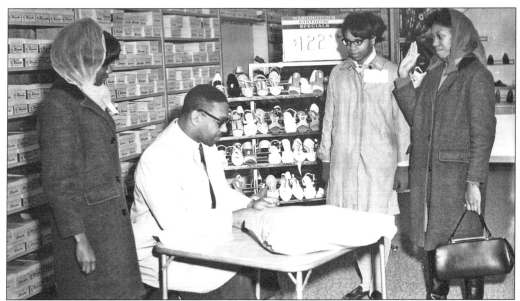

S.D. Harvey, the Urban League's first director, focused on creating more job opportunities for African Americans and implemented a successful job-training program. A downtown store hired its first African American as stockroom clerk, Western Electric hired its first African Americans for technical jobs, and the city hired its first African American as a fireman. Businesses began to look to the Urban League for qualified applicants. The league created a skills bank, which listed individuals with the required education and training to fill the jobs. The Urban League made history by taking the lead in moving qualified African Americans and other minorities into jobs traditionally held by whites. Tom Elijah, pictured below standing, became the director in 1977 and continued to build a network of employment and education programs to serve the increasing number of disadvantaged citizens. (Courtesy of the Winston-Salem Urban League.)

Rev. Moses Alexander Smalls was a community minister. During the early 1970s through the 1980s he operated the Home of Hope on Patterson Avenue across from the old Sealtest Dairy plant, and then later opened in the old southern coal yard on Northwest Boulevard. In addition to his services, he worked with the Black Panthers and offered a free breakfast program, sickle cell testing, and clothing giveaways. (Courtesy of *The Chronicle*.)

Social capitalist Bobby Wilson saw a need in the community and sought to fill it by forming HUMAN Inc. This nonprofit corporation sought to elevate the level of human equality, education, housing, and economic development for the incarcerated, homeless, and disadvantaged. Programs include National Children's Day celebrations, voter education and participation for incarcerated persons, employment and resources for ex-offenders, and art exhibits for inmates. (Courtesy of the Wilson Collection.)

Both Shiloh Baptist Church and St. Peter's World Outreach Center Church had inquired about purchasing the Brown Elementary School for community services. In 1985, the senior pastors, Dr. J. Ray Butler (second from right), and Dr. R.K. Hash (second from left), formed a joint partnership called the Shiloh–St. Peter's Corporation. This photograph shows the founders and first members of the board. (Courtesy of *The Chronicle*.)

The Experiment in Self Reliance (ESR) was chartered in 1964 to eliminate poverty and homelessness. Led by Louise Wilson, their programming included eight community houses in low-income areas to provide a place for residents to freely speak about their needs and problems. Throughout the years, ESR has been a beacon of hope in the community from the war on poverty to welfare reform. (Courtesy of ESR.)

The Best Choice Center was founded in 1988 by the East Winston Restoration Association. Dorothy Graham Wheeler (right) served as the executive director. It was an intervention program for children whose parents had alcohol and substance abuse problems. In 2002, the Best Choice Center became a program of the YWCA. The program continues its academic focus and helps children discover life outside of their neighborhoods. (Courtesy of *The Chronicle*.)

The East Winston Community Development Corporation (CDC) was formed in 1988. James Grace, president, and Rutherford Mormon were early leaders. The CDC completed a low-income housing project called Thirty-Six East. It was the first multifamily low-income housing tax credits project to have central air and washer-dryer connections. The current organization, Neighbors for Better Neighborhoods, came out of a partnership between the CDC and the Winston-Salem Foundation. (Courtesy the Grace Collection.)

A library branch to serve African American residents of Winston-Salem opened on February 15, 1927. For four years, the library was located in the Chestnut Street Branch of the YWCA. The library was named for famous African American poet George Moses Horton. In 1953, Dr. H.D. Malloy Sr., Dr. H. Rembert Malloy, and Dr. J.C. Jordan donated land for a new library facility on East Seventh Street. On November 14, 1954, the library was renamed the East Winston Branch Library. In 1998, the branch was designated as a Heritage Center and on January 12, 2004, the name was changed to the Malloy-Jordan/East Winston Heritage Center. Below is a photograph from The East Winston Branch Library dedication in 1954. Staff members pictured are, from left to right, unidentified, Mary Bruce, Emmaline Goodwin, unidentified, and Nell Wright. (Courtesy of FCPL.)

Bookmobiles started as book wagons in 1905 in the United States to provide traveling library services in rural areas and extended to urban areas. On March 18, 1849, the Forsyth County Public Library purchased its first bookmobile with state aid funds. This 1950s photograph shows the bookmobile from the George Moses Horton Branch Library out in the community. The bookmobile continues to go out into the community today to various daycare centers and teachers are allowed to check out books for their centers. The bookmobile also makes community stops in designated neighborhoods for individuals to check out books. The photograph below was taken at the George Moses Horton Branch Library in 1951. Librarian Mary Henry is seated at right. The others are Hasker Samuels, David Hedgley Jr., Bruce Chaskley, Virginia Hairston, Juanita Braddy, and Alphonzo Cain. (Courtesy of FCPL.)

At left, poet laureate Langston Hughes gives a reading on February 6, 1949, for the Negro History Week Book Fair at the George Moses Horton Branch Library. Below, East Winston Library branch manager (later director) Tim Jackson and librarian Lois Leggett are bar-coding books for the library's automated catalog and circulation system, implemented in 1989. Leggett won a contest naming the process "Grin and Bar It," issued by then outreach director Sylvia Sprinkle-Hamlin, who went on to become the first African American and first female director of the Forsyth County Public Library. (Courtesy of FCPL.)

Chartered in 1924, the Phi Omega chapter of Alpha Kappa Alpha sorority made a conscious decision to do something above and beyond the call of duty. In 1986, a vision formed of building affordable housing in an inner city neighborhood. Motivating factors were quality of life, economic empowerment, continued growth and vitality, and service to all mankind. This vision was to be implemented by the members of the sorority. The sorority used the experience of its membership and their service mindset to construct the Ivy Arms Apartment complex, with valued assets of $2.25 million. The complex includes 44 apartment units and a community center available to organizations. Pictured above are, from left to right, Pat Ford, LaRue Cunningham, Susie Nance, Ladessa Cunningham-Pearson, Maurice Jackson, Jeannette Lewis, and Janet Wheeler. (Courtesy of Janet Wheeler.)

The Rho Zeta chapter of Zeta Phi Beta sorority was chartered in Winston-Salem in 1935. The chapter has established relationships with community organizations, awarded scholarships to student scholars, and has impacted the development of young girls and women through the Archonette and Amicae auxiliaries. The chapter's most precious legacy is the active membership of one of the founders, Pearl Anna Neal, who also served as a chapter president. (Courtesy Zeta Phi Beta Sorority.)

The Winston-Salem chapter of The Links Incorporated was established in 1950. The chapter's purpose is to improve the quality of life through the development and implementation of service projects. Pictured early members are, from left to right, (first row) Lizzie Brandon, Janie Williams, Ethel Wilson, Vern H. Smith, and Louise Davis; (second row) Eleanor Hall, Melanie Walker, Elaine Malloy, Beatrice Jordon, Nell W. Alford, and Irma Todd. (Courtesy of The Links.)

Organized in 1949, the Moles (above) performed service projects to uplift the community. Pictured from left to right are (first row) M. Diggs, M. Wilson, ? Quick, L. Lewis, C. Robinson, G. Ashley, N. Bowman, L. Wilson, M. Poag, and A. Rivea; (second row) E. Fox, Dr. Quick, Dr. McCloud Sr., E. McCloud, I. Williams, M. Hairston, R. Hairston, C. Greenwood, L. Hamilton, A. Noel, T. Poag, F. Wilson, and T. Diggs; (third row) Dr. Noel, P. Rivera, D Wilson, J. Greenwood, J.D. Ashley, C. Hamilton, J. Bauson Jr., and J. Lewis. The Top Ladies of Distinction sponsor the Top Teens of America. The 1987 officers pictured below are, from left to right, (first row) Velma Friende, Manderline Scales, and Vivian Burke; (second row) Elsie Blackman, Jacqueline Dunlap, Carolyn Strickland, Thelma Small, and Dorothy Ross (Above, courtesy of Virginia Newell; below, courtesy of *The Chronicle*.)

The Southeast Region of the National Women of Achievement Inc. was organized by Helen Falls in the 1980s. The organization has several chapters and encourages youth to strive for high moral standards. Pictured above are, from left to right, (first row) Virginia Newell, Joan Cardwell, Helen Falls, Sarah Murray Stephney, and Nancy Wilks; (second row) Manderline Scales, Louise Wilson, Sadie Webster, Thelma Small, Clara Hayes, Constance Johnson, Cordella Rumph, Louise Hamilton, and Roxanna Pitts. Pictured below are, from left to right, Shirley Holloway, Joann Falls, and Annie Hairston; (second row) Ruth Gwynn, Georgia Moore, Edna Revels, Helen Falls, Celenia Nichols, Earnestine Cathcart, and Nell Britton. (Courtesy of *The Chronicle*.)

The Ionic Lodge of the Prince Hall Masons was established in 1895, becoming the first lodge in Winston-Salem. The Prince Hall Masons have five lodges in Winston-Salem, the Ionic No. 72, Salem No. 139, Bivouac No. 503, James H. Young No. 670, and Olympic No. 795. These lodges have been and continue to be pillars of the community working for the betterment of all. Pictured above are the Masons at the symbolic log rising of the African Log Church in Old Salem in 1999. Organized within the Prince Hall Masons, The Order of the Eastern Star (OES) is an affiliate of the Prince Hall Masons which both women and men can join. Pictured below is a 1965 photograph of Meridian Chapter No. 308. In the back row is Jerry Gilmore (left) and worthy matron Lolene McCorkle (wearing black sash). (Above, courtesy of OSM; below, courtesy of the Perry family.)

Sethos Temple No. 170 was organized in 1946 by a group of Masons created as the Shriners in Rameses Temple, which included Clark S. Brown Sr. and Carl H. Russell Sr. The Rameses Shriners organized the Red Fez Club and held their meetings at the Chauffeur Club and operated under the Rameses charter. The organization provides community service projects. Pictured are, from left to right, (first row) John Alexander, Leroy Trotman, Billy Simmons Sr., James Travis, and James Davenport; (second row) Wilson Collins, Michael Williams, George Redd, James McCoy Jr., Donald Christan, and James Chalmers. Pictured below are members of the Camel City Chauffeurs Club. (Above, courtesy of *The Chronicle*, below, courtesy of SSAH.)

A native Liberian, James Hunder formed the Liberian Organization of the Piedmont in 1988 with the mission to advance educational opportunity, human relations, international understanding, and brotherhood. The Liberian Organization hosts special events, often attended by Liberian government officials. Pictured are, from left to right, James Hunder, Luci Vaughn, and Deputy Chief of Liberia Edwin Sele. (Courtesy of the Liberian Organization of the Piedmont.)

Organized in 1957 as Winston-Salem Sportsmen Club of the Patterson Avenue YMCA, the group was an auxiliary club for young male executives and public servants who were former athletes. Today, the club recognizes outstanding athletes through the Winston-Salem/Forsyth County High School Sports Hall of Fame. Pictured are, from left to right, (first row) Albert Poe, Pride Shore, Isaac (Ike) Howard, Fred Douglas, and Foster Lassiter; (second row) Wendell Brown, Willis Miller, Benny McBride, Vic Lawrence, Marshall Hairston, David Plumber, Charlie Clifton, and Howard Ward. (Courtesy of *The Chronicle*.)

The Winston-Salem Alumni Chapter of Kappa Alpha Psi Fraternity Inc. was chartered in 1950. The Kappa Foundation of Winston-Salem Inc. was founded as a nonprofit corporation with the purpose of fostering the intellectual, ethical, social, and moral development of young people, particularly disadvantaged African American young men. The Kappa League, Beautillion Militaire, and Achievement Through Partnership programs serve as the cornerstones of the Foundation's youth initiatives. (Courtesy of Kappa Alpha Psi, Winston-Salem Alumni Chapter.)

Psi Phi chapter of Omega Psi Phi fraternity was chartered in 1932. The Omega Talent Hunt Contest is one of the fraternity's nationally mandated programs, which was founded by local member Jasper Alston (Jack) Atkins. Others programs are Achievement Week, to promote the study of African American life and history, and the Omega Mardi Gras, held to support the scholarship programs. (Photograph courtesy of Galvin Crisp.)

Established in 1923, The Delta Sigma chapter of Phi Beta Sigma adheres to the fraternity motto: "Culture for service and service for humanity." The Sigmas serve the city through active participation with Big Brothers/Big Sisters, the March of Dimes, the cancer walk, and many other worthwhile organizations. The Sigmas' goal is to fulfill community needs through bigger and better business, social action, and education. (Courtesy of Phi Beta Sigma.)

Alpha Pi Lambda chapter of Alpha Phi Alpha Fraternity Inc. was chartered in 1931. The chapter supports the fraternity's national youth-focused partnerships with Big Brothers/Big Sisters, March of Dimes, and Project ALPHA. Activities include the founder's day dance, Martin Luther King Jr. celebrations, college scholarships, and the Bro. Lowden Anderson Science Fair competition. (Courtesy of Alpha Phi Alpha.)

For over a half a century, African American organizations have sponsored pageants to nurture young girls and prepare them for womanhood. Iota Phi Lambda sorority sponsored the Debutante Cotillion in Winston-Salem for more than 33 years. Zeta Phi Beta sorority sponsored the Blue Revue Pageant, a scholarship and educational program that focuses on etiquette, community service, and college preparation for female high school seniors. The Alpha Kappa Alpha sorority presents Fashionetta, which exposes young women to educational, cultural, and social events as well as participation in community service projects. The events culminate with an elegant affair. Delta Sigma Theta sorority sponsors Jabberwock, an evening of elegance and entertainment that showcases the gifts and talents of the young women participating in the program, while promoting scholarship. Above is a 1940s photograph of Vivian Crutchfield and friends. It appears they are dressed for the debutante ball. (Courtesy of SSAH.)

Three

CRAFTSMEN, ARTISTS, AND MUSICIANS

Called the "city of the arts," Winston-Salem's craftsmanship and artistry dates back to the skilled Moravian artisans of the 18th century. Among them was the enslaved African American Peter Oliver, who worked in the pottery shops of the Moravians' master craftsmen. History has overlooked the contributions of most slave artisans; however, Oliver was a skilled potter who earned money from selling ceramics to purchase his freedom. Over a half-century later, a son of former slaves would move to Winston-Salem and gain international fame from the craft of brick making. In the late 20th century, African American artists at Winston-Salem State University produced significant works. The Winston-Salem/Forsyth County schools also provided an avenue for creative expression among its students. An African American student from Carver High School designed the new seal for Forsyth County. In the 1970s, the city's recreation department began presenting African American cultural programs. Later, the program was folded into the Arts Council and called Urban Arts Program with a fulltime director and staff. Under the leadership of Reggie Johnson, Urban Arts would shoulder the responsibility of presenting the work of local and regional trained and self taught African American artists. Visual artists such as Arcenia Davis, Glenda Wharton, Cleveland Wright, James Peck, James Funches, Paul Roseboro, and Lewis Cornell would have a venue to publicly display their work. Photographers set up their studios and captured some of the most compelling images of African American life ranging from christenings to weddings, such as Clarence Nottingham, Howard Ward, and Bobby Gwyn. Then there was Santana (John Acker), who could be found all over Winston-Salem armed with his camera capturing our most candid images. The baton has passed to Ralph Meadows, a community photographer who can be found at civic events capturing moments in time. Winston-Salem is home to some of the greatest musicians in the country. The Five Royales rhythm and blues group is credited with influencing what became known as soul music, including Chris Murrell, a vocalist who performed with the renowned Count Basie Band, Darryl Napper, a musician with national gospel groups, and Hobart Sharpe, a musician with Jeffrey Osborne, and the late Harry Wheeler, Curtis Hairston, and Bernard Foy.

This is a copy of an 1806 letter from the Salem community store Letter Book. Peter Oliver inquired about anticipated payment for good bored pipe stems. This speaks to the quality of his work and his dealings as a businessman. Peter Oliver has many local descendants, including Dr. Raymond Oliver, Shirley Oliver Gibson, Cecil Oliver, Dazelle Benbow Jones, and NBA player Chris Paul. (Courtesy of the Moravian Archives, Winston-Salem, NC.)

Willie H. Johnson Jr.'s design won the contest for the design of a new seal for Forsyth County in 1949. Johnson was a student at Carver High School. The design was placed in the time capsule that was buried on the lawn of the courthouse in 1949. The capsule was removed in 1958 due to courthouse expansion. Here, he is presented with a copy of the resolution proclaiming a new seal for Forsyth County. The other men pictured are James G. Hanes, unidentified, and William B. Simpson. (Courtesy FCPL.)

George Black, the son of a former slave, came to Winston-Salem during the late 1800s. By working at the brickyard of a white brick maker, Black developed his skill and established his own brick making company. He became a sought-after craftsman beginning in the 1920s. His bricks were used in Winston-Salem's finest homes and in churches and businesses. Because he still made bricks by hand using the 18th and 19th century technique, his bricks were used in the restorations of Colonial Williamsburg in 1931 and Old Salem Museums and Gardens in the 1950s. In 1970, Black went to Guyana as a master craftsman and taught brick making. (Courtesy of the George Black Foundation.)

In 1897, George Black married Martha Jean Hampton and they had nine children. In addition to being a great businessman, Black was a family man who valued a strong family unit. In 1934, he moved his family into this house located at 111 Dellabrook Road. In the 1940s, he built a brickyard behind his house. The brickyard operated until the 1970s. The entire site was listed in the National Register of Historic Places in 2000 and in 2011 was designated as a Forsyth County Local Historic Landmark. A historic marker was placed on the property. Below is a photograph of the brickyard restoration. (Courtesy of Triad Cultural Arts.)

Chartered in 1939, the Winston-Salem alumnae chapter of Delta Sigma Theta sorority had an affinity for the arts, which led to the establishment of Winston-Salem Delta Fine Arts Inc. in 1972. It was the city's first nonprofit cultural and educational organization established by African American women. Simona Allen was the founder and served as its first president. The organization established a permanent collection of paintings and sculpture at Winston-Salem State University by acclaimed North Carolina born African American artists. In 1982, the Delta Arts Center was opened in a small house. In 2004, they moved to a new facility on New Walkertown Road. Dianne Caesar is the center's current director. Internationally known artists exhibit at the center and educational arts programs are held throughout the year. Pictured below are sorority members with the Biggers mural gifted to Winston-Salem State University. (Above, courtesy of the Allen family; below, courtesy of the Johnson family.)

Diggs Gallery is named for James Thackeray "T" Diggs Jr., a 1934 graduate of Winston-Salem State University, a painter, and a former art professor for more than 40 years. Seeking to create an art space for "people of all walks of life," Winston-Salem philanthropist Gordon Hanes initiated the creation of Diggs Gallery in 1989. The gallery opened in 1990 and the university has since witnessed tremendous cultural growth through gifts and acquisitions. The unique sculpture garden, Biggers murals, and permanent collection makes Diggs an important regional cultural center, boasting one of the largest exhibition spaces dedicated to the arts of Africa and the African Diaspora in North Carolina. Exhibitions, publications, and programs address a broad range of artistic expressions. Belinda Tate (left) has been the gallery director since 1999. Her predecessors are Hayward Oubre, Mitzi Shewmake, and Brooke Anderson. Tyrone Mitchel's *Po Tolo* is pictured below. (Courtesy of Diggs Gallery, WSSU; photograph by Garret Garms.)

James T. Diggs Jr. is described as a jack-of-all-trades. He was a philosopher, educator, artist, and craftsman. During the 1930s, he took photographs for the "Negro Page" of the *Winston-Salem Journal*. Most known for his paintings, he produced a large body from the 1940s through the 1960s. He was an emeritus professor of art at Winston-Salem State University until he retired in 1969. (Courtesy of Diggs Gallery, WSSU.)

Born in 1908, Vester Lowe was a woodcarver who created a unique collection of carvings that combined both African and European creative traditions. His carvings are considered part of the American folk art tradition, with a major portion of his work being created from 1940 to 1957. Pictured is a photograph of Lowe holding one of his carvings, mounted in a frame that he also carved. (Courtesy of Diggs Gallery, WSSU.)

Hayward Oubre was the chairman of the art department at Winston-Salem State University from 1965 to 1981. He was a wire sculpture artist and was referred to as the master of torque. He corrected the color triangle that was devised by Johann Wolfgang von Goethe and received a copyright for his correction in 1975. (Courtesy of WSSU-CGOL.)

Geraldine Pete, the 1964 class president, is pictured with the ram sculpture that her class presented to C.G. O'Kelly Library during its dedication in 1967 at Winston-Salem State College, now Winston-Salem State University. The wire sculpture was created by Hayward Oubre. (Courtesy of WSSU-CGOL.)

Roland S. Watts served as professor and chairman of the fine arts department at Winston-Salem State University for 39 years. Well-recognized for his extraordinary talent as an artist, he was known across the Southeast as a skilled woodblock printer. He put together 10 one-man exhibitions and participated in 29 group shows in several cities in North Carolina and other states. Above, Prof. Roland S. Watts is pictured at a student art exhibit in January 1966. At right is a print titled *End of a Prayer.* Watt described the bearded priest praying as a vigorous study of a man in communication with his God. Watt's woodcuts were used to express his concern with society, his involvement with fellow men in birth, love, play, frustration, struggle, and the ultimate surrender to death. (Above, courtesy of Winston-Salem State University Archives, C.G. O'Kelly Library; right, courtesy of Watts Collection.)

James (left) and Earnestine Huff, a husband and wife team, created a highly acclaimed body of work that has been exhibited nationally and internationally. The Huffs worked from their home studio on Patterson Avenue and produced art that appeared in more than 25 major publications and periodicals including *Ebony, Encore, Art Voices, Essence, Black Family Magazine*, and the history book *Paths Towards Freedom*. They received the Best in Show award in 10 national art competitions. James designed and produced Nabisco's Famous Black American poster series from 1978 to 1989. In 1990, he was commissioned to design the *Sit-in* sculpture for the Woolworth Museum in Greensboro, North Carolina. For the Huffs, art was a family affair. Their daughter, Jasmine, and son, Quentin, now adults, are both artists. (Courtesy of the Huff Art Studio.)

Jerry Hanes has been creating artwork in the city for over 30 years and works in various mediums. His work, "Hanes Manor," miniature replicas of historic homes, was exhibited in Pride and Dignity from the Hill: A Celebration of the Historic Happy Hill Community at Diggs Gallery in 2011. (Bobby Roebuck photograph courtesy of Jerry Hanes.)

In 1980, Jerry Hanes cofounded the Twin City Art League. The league was established to expose minority artists and their work to the community, to provide support for minority artists, and to help identify unknown artists. Pictured are, from left to right, Jerry Hanes, Charles Hughes, Tony Chisholm, Charles Robinson, George Mack, Ronald Mack, Ronald Ragins, Frank McKissick, and Alvin Kennedy. (Courtesy of Jerry Hanes.)

Leo Rucker is a true community artist who serves his community unselfishly. Being able to create images that touch people's lives has always been his passion. His work has been commissioned by the public and private sector. Working in the mediums of pencil, pastel, acrylics, watercolor, and oils, his artwork is characterized by the photorealism that captures the heartbeat of his subjects. (Courtesy of Leo Rucker.)

Gilbert Everard Young exhibits his work in diverse venues and is always known to make a provocative statement to raise the consciousness of society. His collage art included mirrors so that the viewer was incorporated in the painting. A true community gem, he has developed "state of mind" art stemming from a cosmic and spiritual point of view, which induces respect for another person's point of view. (Courtesy of TCA.)

Barbara Eure is a gifted artist known for her pottery and woodcarvings. She has served with several arts groups, including the Delta Arts Center and Piedmont Craftsmen. In the early 1990s, she served as exhibition coordinator and as a consultant for the CIAA basketball tournament and National Black Theatre Festival. She is a pottery specialist at Summit School and in her home studio she offers summer youth camps and art lessons. (Courtesy of Triad Cultural Arts.)

Bobby Roebuck is a visual artist and photographer. Self-taught, his primary medium, pencil and graphite, bring to paper his unique black and white images. His trademark is detailed abstract drawings featuring geometric shapes and small meticulous dots. Bobby earned a number of awards from associated artists and the Dixie Classic Fair, and has exhibited his works at Salem College, Delta Fine Arts Center, Associated Artists Gallery, and WSSU. (Courtesy of Bobby Roebuck.)

Cornelia Matthews Webster responds artistically to realities in this very black and white America. Her work is a reflection of ethnic and historic visualizations. She believes that African American heritage and culture should not be forgotten and discarded but valued for future generations. In 1980, she developed Sash Art using antique window sashes. Views from her windows can open up mental barriers and help to overcome the invisible walls that divide us. In 1998, she cofounded the first Sit-in Victory Museum with her father, Carl Matthews, who led the city's sit-in movement. The museum was located at 800 North Cameron Avenue in the original home of the late Dr. Joseph Walker Jr., the former president of the Kate Bitting Reynolds Memorial Hospital professional staff. Pictured below is *Alien I's*. (Courtesy of the Webster Collection.)

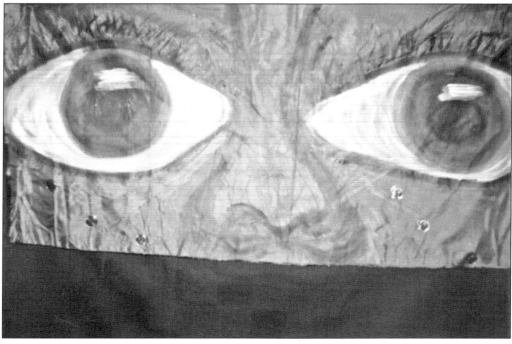

Tahnya Spirit is a visual artist, photographer, published author, and gallery owner. She currently serves as the creative director for the My Natural is Divine planetary movement and foundation. Tahnya's work can be found in private collections nationwide and is on permanent display in the Winston-Salem Downtown Cultural Café. A vast collection of her photography can be viewed at the National Botanical Portrait Museum. (Courtesy of Tahyna Spirit.)

Marvette Pratt Aldrich has been producing rich cultural artwork for many years. She likes to explore the psychological and social impact of racism, sexism, injustice, and ignorance as it relates to black women and women in general. She has participated in several juried shows and has received numerous awards. She is an adjunct art professor at Winston-Salem State University and now creates art full-time. (Courtesy of Marvette Aldrich.)

On July 29, 1948, there was an announcement in the colored section of *the Lexington Dispatch Newspaper* that read, on Monday night at 8:00 p.m., the famous Camp Meeting Choir under the direction of Garfield Wilson would be at the Union Baptist Church. Garfield Wilson (above left) led the famous Camp Meeting Choir well into the 1960s. Wilson also performed with the Royal Sons Gospel Quintet that was formed around 1938. The Royal Sons evolved into the Five Royales. Pictured below are members of the Camp Meeting Choir around 1930 to 1940. Seated on the right is C. Montgomery, who was honored by the NAACP in 1966 for his service as president. (Courtesy SSAH.)

Minister Alvin "AC" Stowe had a rhythmic voice tailored for radio and he spent his life on-air. He worked in the music industry as a program director, promotions manager, producer, and announcer at WAAA and WQMG 97.1. In the community, AC served as the guest host for major concerts and events because of his professionalism, flair, and his keen ability to make your program his. (Courtesy of the Stowe Collection.)

Anita Dean, the "Boss Lady of Gospel," has graced the airways for over 30 years. She got her start at a little station on Northwest Boulevard, becoming the first female radio announcer in this market. She has worked at WEAL, WAIR, and WAAA radio stations and now is the face and the voice of *The Light*. Anita is a mistress of ceremonies for gospel programs. (Courtesy of the Dean Collection.)

The Napper Singers, all sisters, were formerly the Warrenette Gospel Singers, named for their father, Warren. They were organized out of Emmanuel Baptist Church. The group performed traditional gospel throughout the southeast. They have released an album, a 45 record, and a CD. Pictured are, from left to right, (first row) Constance Daniels, Calvin Napper, and Carolyn Napper; (second row) Berlene Smith, Belinda Daniels, and Wynette Napper. (Courtesy of *The Chronicle*.)

The Twin City Choristers, a male chorus, was founded by Dr. Permilla Flack Dunston in 1957. Originally, the Choristers consisted primarily of male high school students from Carver High School, where Dunston taught music. Through the years under various directors, The Choristers have continued to render concerts in and around Winston-Salem and nationally. (Courtesy of The Twin City Choristers; photograph by Bobby Gwyn.)

D' Walla Simmons Burke (right) is the director of choral and vocal studies of the fine arts department at Winston-Salem State University. She is the founder of three of the four choral ensembles within the department, which includes the renowned Winston-Salem State University Burke Singers. Simmons-Burke has conducted with the New England Symphony and Chorale and the Winston-Salem State University Choir at Carnegie Hall. The Winston-Salem State University Choir has performed and recorded with the Dvořák Symphony in Prague, Czech Republic. This recording was nominated in 2010 for a Grammy Award in several categories. Burke is a sacred music and multicultural music clinician, lecturer, and soloist, and serves as a guest conductor and adjudicator for secondary school and collegiate choral festivals and workshops. The original Burke Singers pictured below are, from left to right, Calsine Pitt Jones, Cassandra McCloud-Durant, Temeka McCain, and Sonya Melton. (Courtesy of the Simmons Burke Collection.)

As a recreational director for the City of Winston-Salem, Rodney Sumler (left) used to conduct teen dances at the North Elementary School. This led he and Roy Scales to open the Dungeon Club, a cultural center with live entertainment that featured local and regional bands. Filled to more than the 400-capacity weekly, the Dungeon Club was more than just a nightclub. It was a center that held family reunions, voter registration drives, meet-the-candidate forums, and civic meetings. The club employed six employees, bands weekly, and teenagers for the summer to plan, promote, and work outdoor concerts. Another social institution is Tony's Lounge, founded in 1985 by Tony Couch (below). Tony's was opened as a private club with many of the city's professionals as patrons. (Left, courtesy of *AC Phoenix News*; below, courtesy of the Couch Collection.)

The Eliminators, a rhythm and blues group, was organized in 1967. In 1974, they signed to record with Brunswick Records, a Chicago label that also represented the great Jackie Wilson and The Chi-Lites. Pictured are, from left to right, (first row) Nathaniel Williams, Donald Clark, Levon Myers, and Calvin Westfield; (second row) James Anderson, James Funches, Robert Burroughs, "Rebop" Gordon, Joe Robinson, Carl Johnson, and Clifford Little. (Courtesy of Levon Myers.)

Human Blood was formed in 1973. The rhythm and blues group performed and toured throughout North Carolina. The group disbanded in 1999. Pictured are, from left to right, (first row) Herbert Walters (drums), Francis Wright (vocals), and Herb Stephens (guitarist); (second row) Michael Hammond (keyboardist) and Robert "Apple Jack" Watters (bass). (Courtesy of Herb Stephens.)

Gore and Upsetters was formed in 1958 by Clarence Gore. Many different artists performed with Gore over the years. In 1962, he opened the Gore's Gay 90s Club. It was located on Liberty and Main Streets and was formerly called the Peacock Lounge. People from all across the state of North Carolina would come to his club. Nationally known singers performed there, such as Joe Tex, Chuck Jackson, Solomon Burke, Dionne Warrick, and Joe Simon. Gore's band was on concert tours with Rufus Thomas, Patti Labelle, and the June German Dancers. Pictured below is one of Gore's later bands. (Courtesy of Clarence Gore.)

Bill McClain formed Mr. Bill's Productions while in college. He built a strong clientele and was at every concert, festival, and community function in Winston-Salem. His business as a full-service sound production company spread like wildfire. Now 20 years later, he travels all over the country and provides employment to teens as an alternative to their getting involved in street life. In 1966, Melvin "Schoolboy" Oates organized the Swinging Set jazz band. The band performed for parties and other social functions. Melvin is pictured at the drums. (Right, Courtesy of *The Chronicle*; below, courtesy of the Wachovia Historical Society Collection, photograph courtesy of Old Salem Museums and Gardens.)

The Superiors Band was a leading top 40 and R&B group during the late 1960s and 1970s. The group later evolved to become Opus 7. They toured the country and made several recordings for Great World of Sound, Gram-O-Phon, and Source Records. Pictured are, from left to right, Wendell Robinson, Abdul Rahim Amiyr, Eugene Timmons, Gary Hairston, "Pete" Porter (on microphone), Rudy Anderson Jr., unidentified, and Charles Burns. The Opus 7 Band is pictured below, from left to right, (first row) Galvin Crisp and Gary Harrison; (second row) Wendell Robinson, Sam Hamlin, Rahim Jamal, Charles Burns (in tree), and Harry Austraw. (Above, courtesy of Rudy Anderson; below, courtesy of Galvin Crisp.)

Four

HOME SWEET HOME

The Happy Hill community was the first planned African American neighborhood in Winston-Salem. In May 1872, the Moravian Church laid out streets and lots on the former Schuman Plantation to be sold to freed slaves for home ownership at the asking price of $10. Each lot was 100 feet wide and 200 feet long. The Moravians named the area Liberia. However, the freedmen called the neighborhood Happy Hill and it has retained that name today. In May 2009, a historic marker was placed in Happy Hill to commemorate this historic neighborhood. Black neighborhoods grew during the late 1890s due to the tobacco factories in Winston. In Salem, the main black settlement became Columbia Heights, which was founded in the early 1890s by non-Moravians. Columbia Heights was home to middle-class African Americans and was comprised of the Slater Industrial School, leading black businesses and churches, and better homes. Happy Hill was a small settlement of tobacco workers, laborers, and domestic workers. A number of African Americans lived in Waughtown, a community adjacent to Happy Hill. The first brick house thought to be erected by an African American was owned by Lewis Hege, a Black Moravian who moved from Salem to East Seventh Street. Urban renewal destroyed many early African American neighborhoods. Separated from friends and memories, these resilient descendants of slaves decided to reclaim their past and, in the 1990s, neighborhood reunions began springing up around the city. Former residents gather in parks in the old neighborhoods and spread picnics and reminisce of the good old days when men and women dressed in their finest for church, baths were taken in foot tubs, they went to the corner store to get a pop (soda), and to the Lincoln and Lafayette Theatres to see movies. The Pond Reunion, the Boston Round-up, Belews Street and Vicinity, and Happy Hill Reunion were among the first gatherings. Other neighborhoods such as Piedmont Circle and the West End have formed celebrations. Today, there are still concentrated pockets of Winston-Salem that are exclusively segregated; however, African Americans now live throughout the city creating new home life traditions.

Ned Lemly was a former slave and a member of the African Moravian Church. As a freedman, he became the first homeowner in Happy Hill when he purchased lot no. 1 in 1872. Records indicate that Lemly, who was a farmer, had multiple lots. Georgianna Page is his great granddaughter and is involved in keeping the Happy Hill legacy alive. (Courtesy of the Wachovia Historical Society Collection; photograph courtesy of Old Salem Museums and Gardens.)

Columbus Pitts was an early homeowner in Happy Hill with several lots. He is the grandfather of Maurice Pitts-Johnson who still owns some of his property in Happy Hill. Pitts-Johnson has started a restoration effort of the Happy Hill Cemetery. The gravesites of Columbus Pitts, his wife, Alice, and her mother, Matilda Simmons, along with a number of veteran's graves and others have been restored. (Courtesy of the Wachovia Historical Society Collection; photograph courtesy of Old Salem Museums & Gardens.)

This is a photograph of the senior's club at the old Happy Hill Recreation Center. It was taken in the late 1940s. Pictured in the early 1940s photograph below are children in the old Happy Hill Recreation Center. (Courtesy of the Wachovia Historical Society Collection; photograph courtesy of Old Salem Museums & Gardens.)

Referred to as slums or the ghetto by outsiders, these neighborhoods were home to the people who lived there. For children living in lower-income neighborhoods, playtime was made up from the resources surrounding them. Cardboard boxes became slides, girls made dolls from soda bottles and twine, boys made scooters from old skates, and car tires became swings hanging from a tree. Most kids played outside all day long, moving from street to street and always ending up at a creek. At left is a 1956 photograph of young boys with homemade scooters. Below is a 1950s photograph of two young children standing on a footbridge. (Courtesy of FCPL.)

Most of the low-income houses were shotguns, an architectural style from West Africa. The floor plan in most shotgun houses was very simple. These houses had no hallways so when one entered, they stepped directly into the front room, with a straight shot to the backdoor through the bedroom and kitchen. The front porch was a part of the shotgun house design that had not existed in the United States until the mid-19th century. Shotgun houses were built close together and can be attributed to the kinship found in African American communities, as illustrated below by Lonnie and Hattie Anderson on their front porch. Affluent African Americans resided in middle class neighborhoods such as the Boston Cottages and Columbia Heights. William Shedrick Adams was a grassroots community organizer. He worked to rebuild the historic Reynoldstown neighborhood where he grew up. (Right, courtesy of Ralph Meadows; below, courtesy of FCPL.)

Reynoldstown was developed from 1919 to 1920 by R.J. Reynolds for its black and white workers. In the 1930s it became a predominantly middle-class African American neighborhood. Some of the streets are Cameron, Rich, and Camel Avenues. Other middle class neighborhoods were Columbia Heights, which housed Winston's African American professionals, and Alta Vista, allegedly the first subdivision in the South developed for African American professionals. It was north of the Boston/Thurmond area, bounded by 26th Street to the north, 24 1/2 Street to the south, Cherry Street to the east, and Kirkwood to the west. Above is a photograph of a middle-class home on Cameron Avenue that belonged to Dr. Joseph M. Walker Jr. The current owner has the original doorknocker with Walker's name inscribed. Below is the home of Charles and Irma Gadson, built in 1959 on North Cherry Street by an African American architect. Both images are recent photographs. (Photograph courtesy of Miles Harry.)

A group of members from Union Baptist Church started the Pond Reunion in 1991. The Pond community got its name when the entire wall of the reservoir that overlooked the downward path of North Trade Street collapsed in 1904, which resulted in the area resembling a large pond. Since then, the name "Pond" has been associated with the Trade Street area, which extends over to Seventh Streets and includes streets over to Glenn and Pittsburgh Avenues. The Pond Giants baseball team and the Five Royals R&B Band came out of the Pond. The hang out spot was Haliques Grill owned by H.B. Jones. He was known for his toasted hot dog buns. Pictured above are, from left to right, Delores Scales, Mazie Woodruff, and Rev. B.F. Daniels. (Courtesy of Pond Reunion Committee.)

The Boston Round-up Community Reunion was started in 1993 by Mazie Woodruff. She was inspired by the Pond Reunion, where she was a guest speaker. The committee, led by her daughter, Mildred Strange, held its first reunion at the intersection of University Parkway and North Cherry Street. The city has erected a permanent sign designating the location. The Boston community is comprised of Thurmond Street bound by 25th Street and Northwest Boulevard, North Cherry Street bounded by 14th and 23rd Streets, and smaller streets of 17th Street, Lincoln Avenue, and Pittsburgh Avenue. Three historically black schools still remain in Boston: Kimberly Park and Cook Elementary Schools and Paisley Middle School. Some of the businesses that no longer exist are the Knox Soda Shop, Mr. Ducker's, and several mom and pop stores. Pictured here is Evelyn Carter (far right), the oldest member of the reunion committee. She passed in 2012 at the age of 92. (Courtesy of Mildred Strange.)

Happy Hill Reunion was founded in 1994 by Benjamin Piggott, the director of the William C. Sims Recreation Center in the Happy Hill community and William "Rock" Bitting, a volunteer with the recreation center and former resident of Happy Hill Gardens. The first reunion was held on July 9, 1994, at the Sims Center and Happy Hill Park. In the Happy Hill community there were various businesses, including stores that sold groceries, barbershops, tailors, and an ice cream parlor. Some of the grocers were Jackson Hairston, Dan's place, and Happy Hill Grocery. Bitting Hall was on Pitts Street where meetings were held. The Spot, also known as the Tea Garden, and the Brass Rail provided entertainment. Pictured below are Ben Piggott (left) and William Bitting. (Courtesy of Ben Piggott.)

The Belews Street community reunion started in 1995. In 1958, the Belews Street community was cleared away to make way for US Highway 52. The community included the streets of Belews and Cunningham. Some of the businesses were Othella Beauty Salon, Dave Baity's Barber Shop, James Dixon Grocery, and Linton Cleaners. Pictured above is the reunion committee, from left to right, (first row) Leroy Miller and Barbara Morris; (second row) Harold Springs, Jimmy Jordan, Robert Philips, and Mildred Williams; (third row) Charles Jones. Pictured below are former residents attending a reunion church service at New Hope Baptist Church. (Courtesy of the Morris family.)

Five

EDUCATION AND EXTRACURRICULAR ACTIVITIES

In 1830, North Carolina passed laws that made it illegal to teach African Americans to read and write, largely because of the abolitionist writings encouraging slaves to revolt against their enslavers and also to prevent slaves from forging legal papers to state that they were free. Though many were receiving an informal education at the African Moravian church through Sunday school, when slavery ended, the demand for education by African Americans was amplified. In 1867, African American lay leaders Lewis Hege, Alexander Volger (Gates), and Robert Waugh led the effort to build the first school for African Americans in Salem on land provided by the Home Moravian Church. In Winston, the Depot Street School was opened in 1887 and became the first public school for African Americans. In 1892, Slater Industrial School became the first school to offer high school courses for African Americans. During the early 1900s, Addie C. Morris, a missionary who worked for the Women's Missionary Society, opened a school for children on a lot that was given to her by the First Baptist Church (Highland Avenue). Between 1906 and 1915, the Salem Hill School opened in Happy Hill community. The two-room school was owned by the city and served a wide range of ages up until 1925. Built in 1931, Simon G. Atkins High School became the city's only high school for African Americans. Carver High School, formed from the Oak Grove Junior High School in 1939, was the first county high school for African Americans. In 1959, John W. Paisley High School opened and in 1960 the Columbian Junior High School became a senior high school and was renamed Albert H. Anderson Senior High School in 1962. Schools were not only a place for learning the "three R's," reading, writing and arithmetic, but also provided an outlet for organized extracurricular activities such as plays, music, oratory and debate, choirs, and sports. Later, private and charter schools were established incorporating cultural awareness with academic excellence. Some of the present institutions include the Quality Education Institute, established by the Carver Road Church of Christ in 1992, and the Carter G. Woodson School, which was founded in 1997 by a group of parents led by Hazel Mack.

The first colored school was built in 1867. According to the *People's Press* newspaper, the school was "pleasantly situated in a grove." It was a small white building with plank siding, louvre shutters, and a bell tower. This school filled an educational void for newly freed slaves. The school was located at what is now the intersection of Waughtown and Fayetteville Streets. At the time of the building of the school only 133 of the 116,000 students in North Carolina were African American. Simon Green Atkins established Slater Industrial School in 1892. The photograph below shows a class with Dr. Atkins (center, front row) in front of the brick school that was built in 1895. (Above, courtesy of the Wachovia Historical Society Collection, photograph courtesy of OSM; below, courtesy of Winston-Salem State University Archives, C.G. O'Kelly Library.)

The Memorial Industrial School was born out of a need to fill the void when the Colored Baptist Orphanage, which was formed in 1905, was under financial hardship. A year after it had opened as a school in 1923, it was moved from its location on Main Street to farmland north of the city to serve as an orphanage and learning institution. (Courtesy of SSAH.)

Primary school Columbia Heights opened in 1905 with Dr. Simon Green Atkins as its first principal. In 1923, all high school courses were moved from the Slater Academy to Columbia Heights. Pictured here is the 1948 Columbia Heights primary class. (Courtesy of SSAH.)

The Fourteenth Street School opened in 1924. In 1944, John Ashley became principal of the school and led it to become an esteemed learning institution. Ashley is attributed with introducing instruments into the music program. Pictured at left in this c. 1940 photograph are students of the Fourteenth Street School. (Courtesy of SSAH.)

In 1982, Earline Parmon founded the Lift Learning Center and Academy (Learning Is Fun Too), where students who were considered to be at risk were given a second chance to excel. She served as executive director until the academy closed in 2001. In 2008, a scholarship fund was established in her honor. Parmon has served on the Forsyth County Board of Commissioners and as a North Carolina state representative. (Courtesy of Triad Cultural Arts.)

The 1969 Atkins High School Debating Society is pictured above. From left to right are (first row) C. Bohannon, S. Wilkins, A. Crockette, C. Jeffries, and A. Johnson; (second row) M. Thomas, J. Payne, P. Reynolds, W. Hairston, and J. McMillian; (third row) S. Rawls, G. Philips and R. Woods. At right are the most studious seniors, Ronald Toppin and Cassandra Matthews. (Courtesy of the Huntley Collection.)

The 1969 Atkins High School championship basketball team starting five is pictured here. From left to right are, (first row) Steve Joyner and Michael Copeland; (second row) Teddy East, Cecil Bradshaw, and Gregory Noble. The team had a perfect season, winning 23 straight games. The Atkins All City County players were Cecil Bradshaw and Willie Griffin. (Courtesy of the Huntley Collection.)

High schools had physical education programs to develop students physically as well as mentally. All students were issued gym suits just like they were issued books. The suits had to be turned in at the end of the school year. This also gave instructors an opportunity to discuss cleanliness and personal hygiene. (Courtesy of the Huntley Collection.)

The 1969 Anderson High School senior officers pictured here are, from left to right, (seated) Oscar Bea (vice president) and Aldine Grimes (president); (standing) Brenda West (treasurer), Hubert Jefferies (reporter), Beverly Wallace (assistant secretary), and Jacqueline Bitting (secretary). (Courtesy of Anderson Alumni Association.)

The 1966–1967 Anderson Bulldogs football team had a 6–3–1 record. Pictured are the seniors, from left to right, (first row) N. Williams, N. Brown, S. Alexander, W. Livingston, E. McCorkle, and F. Byers; (second row) T. Foster, T. Samuels, J. Meredith, O. Dunlap, and D. Woods. (Courtesy of Anderson Alumni Association.)

The 1969 Anderson High School future medical workers learned about the medical professions through study, tours, and lectures. Pictured are, from left to right, (kneeling) R. Thomas, J. Lewis, A. Johnson, G. Neal, C. Moore, and P. Jackson; (standing) M. Litaker, C. Harris, I. McGee, R. Penn, Q. Pringle, B. Vance, C. Neal, G. Dixon, S. Carter, R. Burns, D. Wilson, M. Forbes, L. Estes, and J. Miles. (Courtesy of Anderson Alumni Association.)

The 1964 Anderson High School dance group performed various dances that highlighted history, spirituality, and culture. Pictured from left to right are B. Foster, E. Isom, L.Estes, C. Bess, L. Bess, M. Havner, R. Burns, D. Austin, N. McGill, and W. Hedrick. (Courtesy of Anderson Alumni Association.)

Pictured here are members of the 1967 Carver football team, from left to right, (first row) Henry Hawkins, Sam Shelf, Isaac Howard, Harold Jackson, James Turner, Ralph Barber, Steve Bell, and Tim Sullivan; (second row) Daniel Feaster, Bobby Lilly, James Tatum, Lorenzo Peason, Larry Hairston, Willie Pearson, and John Sturdivant; (third row) Donnell Oliver, Harry Treasure, Willie Hairston, Donald Thomas, Herman Martin, Kenneth Park, George Young, and Steve Miller; (fourth row) Franklin Wilson, Sandy Paine, Hoyt Allen, James Isom, Kenneth Havender, Dwight Jones, and Nelson Williams; (fifth row) Coach D.L. Lash, Phillip Melton, Russell Covington, James Hairston, Donald Moore, George Simmons, and Terry Anderson. (Courtesy of Carver Alumni.)

The Carver High School Exclusives, pictured in this 1967 photograph, focused on civic duty. Pictured are, from left to right, Wilhelmia Bitting, Beunice Bradley, Jacquelyn Bigby, Charisse Canady, Josephine Hairston, Jamie Transou, Carole Ferrell, and Elwille Jarrett. (Courtesy of Carver Alumni.)

The 1967 Carver High School Cafeteria Core pictured here are, from left to right, (first row) Jamona Cason, Nicole Shelton, Alease Manns, Wanda Summers, Sheila Brooks, Josephine Hairston, Yetter Jones, Lorraine Watkins, and Shirley Blackmon; (second row) Jerry Matthews, Bertha Hyman, Delane Jessup, Wilhemina Bitting, Jennifer Hart, Irma Bivens, Daniel Feaster, and Janis Shelton; (third row) James Tatum, Barbara Bailey, and Ronald Cook. (Courtesy of Carver Alumni.)

Pictured here is the 1967 Carver High School HI-Y club. From left to right are (first row) Donnell Oliver, Henry Harkins, William Peterson, Roger Haith, Ray Anthony, Hardin Wheeler, Herman McCoy, and Windford Miller; (second row) Claude Hardin, Cornelius Speas, Walter Totten, Calvin Matthews, Michael Mitchell, Curtis Brooks, Allen Speas, and Eugene Baskin; (third row) Clarence Grier, Lindy Palmer, Phillip Milton, Hobart Jones, James Cruchfield, Phillip Littlejohn, David Thomas, and Herman Martin. (Courtesy of Carver Alumni.)

The 1965 Paisley 100 Marching Band was led by Bernard T. Foy. The band was made up of music students from the seventh through twelfth grades. The band performed at halftime of the football games and marched in parades in Winston-Salem and other cities. (Courtesy of Paisley Alumni.)

The 1968 Paisley High School cheerleaders are, from left to right, Shirley Graham, Emogene Cobb, Vernell Hughes, Gwendolyn Black, Rita Richardson, Jacqueline Morrison (kneeling), Sandra Wilson, Senthia Sywgert, Deborah White, and Eather Sims. (Courtesy of Paisley Alumni.)

The 1965 Paisley High School tennis team included, from left to right, (first row) Jacqueline Cardwell, Glenda Cardwell, Josette Keit, Alvita Archie, Conita Archie, and Phyillis Thomas; (second row) Sterling White, Luther Flynt, Charles Miller, Gerald Scott, and Freddie Green. (Courtesy of Paisley Alumni.)

The 1968 Paisley football team included, from left to right, (first row) Charles Bellinger, Victor Thomas, David Rice, Jerry Gillespie, George Poindexter, Charles Archie, Reginald Campbell, Willie Rush, and Ronnie Amason; (second row) Alfred Carter, Darryl Wright, Robert Noble, Charles Hay, Thomas Foggie, Edwin Allen, Charles Bailey, Jason Caldwell, and Horace Bonner; (third row) Antonio Jackson, Michael Alexander, Jerry George, Gregory Noble, John Miller, Calvin Scales, Robert Sockwell, and Ronnie Douthit; (fourth row) Larry Turner, Nathaniel Green, Borris Moses, John Covington, Paul Hay (manager), and Charlie Joe (trainer). (Courtesy of Paisley Alumni.)

In 1945, the Winston-Salem State Teachers College Alumni Association took total control of the homecoming plans. Among the activities was a gala parade. The instruments for the first college band were purchased through a fundraiser by the alumni association. Pictured are, from left to right, drum major Romie Avery and drum majorettes Mary O'Neil, Ann Reynolds, Ruby Watson, and Margie Wells. Below are Girl Scout and Boy Scout troops participating in the 1945 parade. (Courtesy of Winston-Salem State University Archives, C.G. O'Kelly Library.)

Members of the Cosmopolitan Club, a student organization at Winston-Salem Teachers College, rode in a horse-drawn wagon during the 1945 parade. Most of the student organization participated in the parade. Everyone attended the Winston-Salem Teachers College homecoming football game, which was the social event of the year. It called for a new outfit because everyone was dressed to impress. Pictured below is Barbara Spaulding Hayes, the 1955 homecoming queen and her court. Barbara is in the center wearing a crown and Dr. Francis L. Atkins, president of the college, is seen on the far right. Everyone in Winston-Salem was involved somehow in the Winston-Salem State University homecoming events. The parades continue to draw thousands of spectators and hundreds of entries from community organizations. (Courtesy of Winston-Salem State University Archives, C.G. O'Kelly Library.)

The Winston-Salem Christmas Parade was another anticipated event that brought everyone downtown. It was a joyous time for family and friends. Daycare centers and youth groups from the YMCA and the YWCA participated. A term that was coined during the parade was "show out." At a certain point along the parade route, the youth steppers and drummers would halt the parade and put on a show for the spectators. It was the highlight of the parade. Of course, the parade was a great way to advertise businesses as well. Students from Russell's Commercial School are pictured above in 1965. The stenographic school was operated by Lois Russell. (Above, courtesy of Jo Ann Brown; below, courtesy of FCPL.)

The alumni associations of Paisley, Atkins, Carver, and Anderson High Schools combined their annual reunions in the early 1990s and began celebrating together. This event became known as the Big Four Reunion and includes a teacher's luncheon where all the remaining teachers from the schools are honored, along with a worship service, a basketball game, and a dance. Pictured here are photographs from a teacher's luncheon. Above are, from left to right, Billie Matthews (former teacher), Clevelle Roseboro (former student), and Marie Burney (teacher). Below are, from left right, Geraldine McClam Jackson, Carl McLaurin, Eric Martin, George Johnson, Karen Parker, and Bishop Joseph Lowery. (Above, courtesy of Miles Harry; below, courtesy of *The Chronicle*.)

People come from near and far to celebrate the Big Four Reunion weekend. Pictured here are alumni attending the big four dance. Above are, from left to right, (first row) Doris Epperson Griffin, Deborah Ford Sims, and Sharon Howell; (second row) Kenneth Woodruff and Samuel Richardson. Enjoying a dance below are Nathaniel Fleming (left) and Georgia Smith. (Photograph courtesy of Miles Harry.)

The Big Four Reunion always includes a worship service. Pictured above is the lighting of the memorial candle in honor of deceased classmates by Theodis Foster. Below is the infamous Big Four Choir, comprised of members of all four high schools, including Paisley, Atkins, Anderson, and Carver, under the direction of Eddie Bines Jr. (Photograph courtesy of Miles Harry.)

Six

SERVICE, PROTESTS, AND CIVIL RIGHTS

The quest for life, liberty, and the pursuit of happiness has been a hard-fought battle. Slavery's demise in 1865 did not end racism and second class citizenship for African Americans. A racial disturbance that began in March 1895 is an indication of this. A black man was killed by a white policeman, who was found not guilty in spite of eyewitness testimony. Two months later in May, the victim's brother, 19-year-old Arthur Tuttle, was among a group of African American men that officers had asked to clear the sidewalk so that a white woman could pass through. They all did except Tuttle. According to the police report, Tuttle remarked that he would move "when he got damn ready." A fight ensued and Tuttle emerged with a gun and fatally shot a policeman. Charged with second-degree murder, there was apparent concern for Tuttle's safety because he was put on a train and sent to the Guilford County Jail in Greensboro and later moved to the Mecklenburg jail in Charlotte. In August he was returned to Winston-Salem for his trial and the rumor erupted that he was going to be lynched. That is when around 20 African Americans armed with shotguns loaded with bird shot surrounded the jail to protect him. The papers reported that 300 to 500 African Americans gathered at the jail; however, that number is disputed by historians who feel the number was a lot lower. When told to disperse and go home by the mayor and sheriff, the crowd remained. The mayor brought in a well-trained militia group, the Forsyth Rifles, and gave them instructions to fire to hit, which they followed. According to the paper, the encounter lasted four hours. It is interesting that the paper reported that some of the militia received flesh wounds, but did not report whether any of the blacks were killed or injured. Tuttle was sentenced to two years in prison. It is thought that he had retaliated against the police to vindicate his brother's death. Tuttle and the men who went to protect him that night on August 11, 1895, were the forerunners of freedom fighters in Winston-Salem.

Clarence "Pete" Page, a resident of the Happy Hills community, served in the 326th Service Battalion, Quartermaster Corps. Page (seated) and three African American soldiers are pictured. Serving in segregated troops, African American soldiers were treated as second-class citizens even though they fought valiantly for their country. Several acts of bravery by African American soldiers went unrecognized. Pictured below is a parade of colored soldiers on Liberty and Sixth Streets around 1918 to 1920. In the *New York Age*, an influential black newspaper, an article ran on Saturday, April 19, 1919, about the colored people of Reidsville, North Carolina, celebrating Lincoln's birthday. It was reported that there was a "spectacular parade led by the Winston-Salem band and a large number of returned colored soldiers." (Collection of the Wachovia Historical Society, courtesy of OSMG.)

Ralph R. Morgan (right) was a prominent African American leader and World War I veteran. After being wounded in combat, he received the Purple Heart and returned to civilian life where he worked as a chauffeur for a short time before opening a grocery store in the Columbia Heights community. He became state marshal with the American Legion when it was formed in 1919. He held the position of drum major for the Drum and Bugle Corps at his post. Morgan, along with his brother and other community leaders, initiated a plan to own and operate the country's first African American city bus company, the Safe Bus Company. The local American Legion was named in his honor and on October 18, 1957, the Ralph R. Morgan Post 220 was chartered. The post has continued to provide service to veterans, their families, and the community. Below are the 1986 officers Commdr. Larry O. Wilson (left) and Adj. Preston Webb. (Courtesy of Ralph R. Morgan, Post 220.)

Lawrence Joel served in the US Army in both the Korean War and the Vietnam War. While serving in Vietnam as a medic, Joel received the Silver Star and the Medal of Honor for his heroism in a 1965 battle. He was the first living black American to receive this medal since the Spanish-American War in 1898. In February 1986, the Winston-Salem Board of Aldermen voted to name the city's new arena the Lawrence Joel Veterans Memorial Coliseum in his honor. Joel was born in Winston-Salem and attended Atkins High School. He died in 1984 and is buried in Arlington National Cemetery. Above, he and his wife, Dorothy, are pictured at a luncheon in his honor as a Congressional Medal of Honor recipient. At left, children watch a parade held in his honor in 1967. (Courtesy of FCPL.)

The struggle for decent wages and benefits led to protests at Piedmont Leaf Tobacco Company and R.J. Reynolds Tobacco Company. In the summer of 1946, 22-year-old Margaret DeGraffenreid was among the strikers of the Piedmont Leaf plants on Fourth Street. At the time, she was pregnant and had a child at home. According to the police account, DeGraffenreid was resisting arrest; however, she stated that she was pulled out of the line, dragged, and thrown into the police car. The leaf house strike ended in September with a compromise on wages and a significant victory for seasonal workers. They gained three paid holidays, which were the Fourth of July, Labor Day, and Christmas. Pictured above are Police Chief John Gold (right) and Margaret DeGraffenreid. Below, factory workers strike at the R.J. Reynolds plant on Vine Street in 1947. Velma Hopkins was one of the great organizers in the strikes against Reynolds. (Courtesy of FCPL.)

In 1957, 15-year-old Gwendolyn Bailey was the first African American to enroll in an all-white school in Forsyth County. She was not only ostracized at school but also had to endure harassment from whites riding by her house on trucks touting guns. At left, she is photographed entering R.J. Reynolds High School with Velma Hopkins and Harvey Johnston. (Courtesy of *Time & Life Magazines*, FCPL.)

Norma Corley and Roslyn and Kenneth Cooper were the first African American children to integrate an elementary school in Winston-Salem. More than half of Easton's 600 students stayed at home that first day in 1958. Pictured in this 1958 photograph are, from left to right, Lovie Cooper, Kenneth Richard Cooper, Norma Ernestine Corley, Roslyn Dianne Cooper, and Ernest Corley. Frank Jones is in the foreground. (Courtesy of FCPL.)

"PASSIVE RESISTANCE"—Carl Matthews (second from right), joined by sympathizers, sits at a lunch counter in Winston-Salem to protest the lack of sitdown service for Negro patrons of the store.

Staff Photo

Sit-Down Strike Spreads To Twin City and Durham

On February 8, 1960, Carl Wesley Matthews sat down alone at the S.H. Kress lunch counter, which began the sit-in movement in Winston-Salem. On February 23, 1960, 11 African American students at Winston-Salem Teachers College and 10 white students at Wake Forest joined the protest. From Winston-Salem Teachers College were Royal Joe Abbitt, Everette L. Dudley, Deloris M. Reeves, Victor Johnson Jr., William Andrew Bright, Bruce Gaither, Jefferson Davis Diggs III, Algemenia Giles, Donald C. Bradley, Lafayette Cook, and Ulysses Grant Green; from Wake Forest were Linda Cohen, Linda Guy, Margaret Ann Dutton, Bill Stevens, Joe Chandler, Don Bailey, Paul Watson, Anthony Wayland Johnson, George Williamson, and Jerry Wilson. On May 25, 1960, Winston-Salem became the first city in North Carolina to desegregate its lunch counters. Matthews was the first African American to be served at a desegregated lunch counter. He also initiated and financed the first Freedom Ride of the 1960s to allow African Americans to sit where they chose on Grey Line buses. He also initiated the breakdown of rear seat segregation in the courtrooms of Winston-Salem and led the first successful demonstration to open up restroom facilities for Negro women in downtown Winston-Salem. (Courtesy of the Matthews Collection.)

Spurred by Dr. Martin Luther King Jr.'s Selma to Montgomery march, 520 Winston-Salem State College students marched in silence from the campus on Martin Luther King Jr. Drive to the post office on West Fifth Street with no incidents. Many of the students had never participated

in a nonviolent demonstration prior to the march. The students had been instructed to obey all traffic regulations and to proceed in an orderly manner. This panoramic image shows participants in the protest gathered in front of the post office in 1965. (Courtesy of FCPL.)

During the Civil Rights Movement, students from Winston-Salem State College (named Winston-Salem State University in 1969) were active in protests sparked by national and local events. On Sunday, March 21, 1965, students from Winston-Salem State College participated in a sympathy march as a salute to the marchers in Selma, Alabama, who began a 54-mile, five-day walk to Montgomery, Alabama, on the same day. In Montgomery, local citizens, the Student Nonviolent Coordinating Committee, and the Southern Christian Leadership Conference had been campaigning for voting rights. Pictured in these 1965 photographs are students marching from the campus to the post office on West Fifth Street in downtown Winston-Salem. When the students arrived, they united in prayer and song. (Courtesy of FCPL.)

A Cold Day, but a Warm Start
Panthers Serve Eggs, Bacon and Grits

Journal, Thursday, Nov. 6, 1969

David DuBuisson
Staff Reporter

...s cold, maybe 4 0 ... when we got there. ...ifth Street, the sun was ...nning to reflect off the ...dows of the Winston Life Insurance C o.

...lapidated store front ...ered with posters and ... The paint was peeling ...some dim era of East ...eet history. The door ... cracked.

...the air was warm, ...rmer than the greet-... were polite. Two or ...ing black men sat ...eading, while four or ...ouple of children did ... to stay out of the

Times a Week

...s Black Panther ...ers, and we had been ... have a look at their ...akfast for Children ... The breakfasts, now ...sday, Wednesday and ...ave been a long time ... The Panthers are ...the project — proud ...o overcome their ... dislike for being ...ed.

...are vague with the ...here and elsewhere. ...donate money and ...for the program, ...won't say which ...and they won't say ...or how much. Some ...black and white, ...going rate is $5 a ...se Panthers provide ...envelopes.

...s willing to talk ...many aren't — deny ...at they have been ... down" by the ...at least not so overtly ...ould be considered ...Some have reported

police; none has taken out a warrant.

Robert T. Greer, titular head of the group, says, "You don't have to threaten people for a good cause. "Larry Little, the lieutenant minister of information, likes to describe the appeal as a sort of poor man's United Fund.

Whatever the source, covered trays of scrambled eggs and bacon, racks of milk and a steaming pot of grits were coming in by 7 a.m. Still, few children were there. We wondered if this handful, some obviously the offspring of the providers, would be the sum of it.

We asked.

"Wait till about 7:30," we were told. Still a little reserved, the hosts seemed to be taking our presence for granted now.

Tide of Children

In a minute, the door opened with a blast of cold air. In flowed Defense Captain Greer and Miss Jacqueline Peoples, a prominent Panther "sister" on a tide of children.

The sister eyed the man with the camera carefully and coldly, not certain whether he was to be welcomed or not.

There followed a short, whispered conference at the back, then Miss Peoples, chairman of the breakfast program, approached the reporter. "Who's your brother?" she asked. Told he worked for the newspaper, not the police, she said "okay."

Greer greeted us quickly and dashed off to work.

Business was picking up. Carloads of children arrived at intervals. They are picked up in their neighborhoods by Panther drivers. (One was arrested last week for "blowing his horn unnecessarily"). Others came on foot, in little ...

In the cramped back room, children were eating in shifts, 13 at a sitting. Each got a paper plate of eggs and grits, two strips of bacon, a slice of bread and a half-pint of milk.

"We won't just give them cold cereal and an apple," Little had said back in September. At the time, the Panthers were looking for the use of a church hall for the breakfasts. They still are.

The breakfast project is not original with Winston-Salem Panthers, who do not constitute a chapter or branch of the national Black Panther party. Panther groups from Berkeley to Boston are doing it. The Nov. 1 issue of The Black Panther newspaper claims that 20,000 children were fed by the Panthers last school year.

Not Far Off

The number, if yesterday's session was typical, may not be far off. By 7:45, the East Fifth Street office was teeming with children. Two of the women and one or two of the young men kept the food coming. Others stayed up front entertaining the children who were waiting to eat or waiting for a ride to school.

Half an hour later, when the rush was over, the woman who had supervised the feeding was asked for a count. She disappeared for a minute, then came back and said, "I started with 100 paper plates and I have 30 left." As she said it, the door opened and five more youngsters headed toward the tables.

Critics, including the police, have said that the breakfasts are a pretense for radical political indoctrination.

If it is, it was well-camouflaged yesterday. True, the walls are plastered with quotations from Mao ("All Power Comes From the Barrel

See Black P. 16 Col. ?

Staff Photo by J...

Donald Snow helps children with breakfast.

In the summer of 1969, the Winston-Salem chapter of the Black Panther Party became a reality with former aldermen Larry Little and Nelson Malloy at the forefront. Although the group sprang from a militant agenda against racism, the organization was very concerned about the plight of some of Winston-Salem's poorest residents and initiated service programs in the community. In 1969, the Panthers implemented the Free Breakfast for Children program chaired by Jacqueline Peoples. Pictured here, Donald Snow assists with serving breakfast. On August 27, 1972, at a Survival Day Rally, groceries and shoes were distributed and voter registration and free sickle-cell anemia tests were held. On January 30, 1974, the Black Panthers started the People's Free Ambulance Service, which functioned 24 hours a day while in operation. On October 14, 2012, a historic marker was placed on the corner of Martin Luther Jr. Drive and Fifth Street. (Courtesy of the *Winston-Salem Journal*.)

In times of crisis, citizens, politicians, ministers, and community organizations have always banded together to fight inequities and injustices. Churches became the venue of choice to organize rallies, hold forums, and conduct voter registration drives. In 1984, the city rallied to support Darryl Hunt, who was wrongfully convicted of a murder he did not commit. The Darryl Hunt Defense Committee, founded by Larry Little, helped to raise several thousand dollars to pay for a private investigator and expert witnesses and a jury selection expert. Hunt was exonerated 19 years later. Pictured above from left to right are (first row) Nelson Malloy, Larry Womble, and Larry Little; (second row) Joycelyn Johnson, Virginia Newell, two unidentified, Earline Parmon, Rev. J. Drayton, and Rev. J. Mendez. Below are journalists Patricia Degraffinreaidt and Jim Steele covering the Minister's Conference's press conference concerning the Darryl Hunt trial. (Courtesy of *The Chronicle*.)

Seven

LIBERATION THROUGH THEOLOGY

Sam, an enslaved African purchased by the Moravian Church, was the first person baptized in the new Salem church in November 1771. Eventually, many more enslaved African Americans would join the church. It is believed by some that many of those enslaved may have joined the Moravian Church in an effort to receive more humane treatment and to escape the cruelty and harshness of slavery. Fittingly, it would be from a church that the enslaved people in and around the town of Salem would hear the announcement of slavery's demise. The church has always been a driving force in the African American community. From the pulpit, black ministers could spread messages of hope and empower and educate their members on economic, political, and social issues. Ultimately, ministers became the power brokers because they had the ear of the black community. The preachers were the only group that was not indebted to the white power structure and did not have to worry about any economic, political, or job-related backlash. Black ministers are responsible for many of the gains that African Americans have obtained, particularly during Reconstruction when they challenged the Jim Crow laws, and during the Civil Rights Movement. In the early 1980s, new young ministers were coming to Winston-Salem to pastor churches. In the past, black ministers had worked with the city's white power structure to maintain peaceful race relations through negotiation. However, the new ministers presented a new style to address race relations and it was a confrontational, "in your face" method. Anyone seeking to get their message into the black community made a stop at the minister's conference, now led by these young ministers. The new millennium ushered in another wave of young ministers who were pastoring in a post-modern culture that changed the face of ministry in the city. Men's and women's empowerment conferences replaced Men's and Women's Day programs. Dress down replaced dressing up for worship, mass media replaced "each one, reach one," and ministerial autonomy became the norm instead of the exception. Always responding to the ever changing times, the church remains the most formidable cultural institution in the African American community.

The African Moravian Church was established in 1822 in Salem (Winston-Salem). The congregation moved from its 1823 log church to a newly constructed brick church in 1861. The St. Philips African Moravian Church is the oldest standing African American church in North Carolina and home to the only historic Black Moravian congregation in the United States. It was from the pulpit of this church that a Union cavalry chaplain announced freedom to the enslaved

community on Sunday, May 21, 1865. After the Civil War, the church served as the focus of the African American community for educational and social functions as well as religious services. The congregation held its last service in the church in 1952 and moved into the Happy Hill community. In 2003, the restored historic church opened again for worship and touring in Old Salem Museums and Gardens. (Courtesy of OSMG; photograph by Christine Rucker.)

The Rev. Dr. Cedric Rodney was the first ordained minister of African descent to pastor the St. Philips Moravian Church from 1968 to 1976 and 1984 to 2003 at its Bon Air Avenue location. He led the efforts to have the historic St. Philips Church in Old Salem restored. He is pictured here receiving an award from Cheryl Harry at the 150th anniversary celebrating the consecration of the 1861 church on December 15. In the background behind Dr. Rodney is Lee French, former president of Old Salem Museums and Gardens. Seated on the front pew are program participants Sophia Foster (left) and Mary Brunson. Less than a year later, on November 26, 2012, Dr. Rodney became the first black Moravian buried in the Moravian God's Acre cemetery in nearly 200 years. (Courtesy of OSMG; photograph by Christine Rucker.)

The pastors of the five churches that were a part of St. Philip's 120th anniversary in 1942 were on the program for the 150th celebration, including Union Baptist Church. Those historical relationships were reestablished after 30 years. Pictured above are, from left to right, (first row) Rev. Donald Jenkins, pastor of St. Paul United Methodist Church; and Rev. Darryl Aaron, pastor of First Baptist Church; (second row) Dr. Sir Walter Mack Jr., pastor of Union Baptist Church; Rev. Stacy Frazier, pastor of Friendship Baptist Church; and Rev. William Brown, pastor of Rising Ebenezer Baptist Church. Not pictured are Rev. Prince Rivers, pastor of United Metropolitan Baptist Church, and Rev. Ronnie Roseboro, pastor of St. Andrews United Methodist Church. Pictured below is Larnethia McConnell Hunter of the North Carolina Liturgical Dance Network. (Courtesy of OSMG; photograph by Christine Rucker.)

On May 5, 1930, at 11:00 a.m., Dr. R.M. Pitts Sr., pastor of the Shiloh Baptist Church, called together all of the Baptist ministers and local preachers for the purpose of organizing a Baptist Ministers Conference. Initially, the conference was designed to promote Christian fellowship among the ministers; however, due to racial injustices, the Ministers Conference was thrust into the role of community leadership. In 1969, Dr. A.H. McDaniel introduced the Four Churches worship service to break down religious barriers. The organizing ministers were D.W. Browning of St. John CME, Dr. Sir Walter Mack Sr. of Emmanuel Baptist Church, and Dr. Jerry Drayton of New Bethel Baptist Church. Today, the Ministers Conference is ecumenical. During the 1980s, Dr. Serenus Churn of the Mt. Zion Baptist Church served as president of the Ministers Conference. The Martin Luther King Day march, breakfast, and scholarship were added to their programs. Pictured above is the Ministers Conference around 1940, and below is Dr. Serenus Churn. (Above, courtesy of the Ministers Conference; below, Mt. Zion Baptist Church.)

Winston-Salem was taken by storm when two northern preachers came to town in the 1980s. Dr. Carlton Eversley came in 1982 and later became pastor of the Dellabrook Presbyterian Church. Dr. John Mendez came in 1984 to pastor Emmanuel Baptist Church. Drs. Eversley and Mendez, both well-known social justice ministers, worked together for freedom, justice, and equality. Their voices resonated through the corridors of city hall, through the chambers at school board meetings, and through the downtown streets of the Twin City. Among other things, Eversley is credited with the formation of a citizens review board by the city council and blocking the resegregation of the school system. Dr. Mendez (below) pulled together an ecumenical cadre to rally against the Ku Klux Klan, who are across the street out of view. (Above, courtesy of Eversley Collection; below, courtesy of the Mendez Collection.)

An international missionary, Dr. Patricia Bailey is a descendant of Timothy, an enslaved African Moravian from Guinea, West Africa. For more than 32 years in over 134 countries around the world she has provided aid and relief to poverty- and famine-stricken peoples. Her school and office, Masters Touch Ministries International, is headquartered in Winston-Salem. (Courtesy of Masters Touch Ministries International.)

In 1988, Bishop Sheldon McCarter became pastor of one of the now largest African American churches in the city. He brought a new paradigm in church worship service and ignited a renewed energy in ministry. His noon Bible study crossed denominational barriers and allowed worshippers to come together regardless of affiliation. Hundreds of people from across the city would gather for a mid-day message and lunch. (Courtesy of Greater Cleveland Avenue Christian Church.)

Civil rights leader Dr. Martin Luther King Jr. made two visits to the city. First to Wake Forest University on October 11, 1962, where he received a standing ovation from an audience of over 2,200 black and white attendees. He ended his speech calling for "black men and white men to join hands together," which became a part his renowned "I Have a Dream" speech. On April 13, 1964, Dr. King spoke at Goler Metropolitan Church. The NAACP and CORE's founder, Dr. James D. Ballard, invited Dr. King to assist with a voter registration drive. Even though a storm delayed his arrival, over 1,000 people waited patiently at the church. (Courtesy of Wake Forest University Archives.)

Martin Luther King Address Scheduled

The Rev. Martin Luther King Jr. will be on campus Thursday night for an address in Wait Chapel.

King, whose appearance is being sponsored by the College Union Lecture Committee, will speak at 8 p.m.

The Negro leader has been called the "symbol today of the fight to end segregation."

He first became involved in desegregation activities in 1955 when he was instrumental in leading a bus boycott in Montgomery, Ala. A majority of the city's 50,000 Negroes participated in the boycott, which ended after a federal court desegregation order.

Soon after the boycott he published a book entitled "Stride Toward Freedom."

King has been arrested and jailed on a number of occasions for violation of anti-trespass laws during sit-in demonstrations. An organization which he heads, the Southern Christian Leadership Conference, sponsored a number of the restaurant sit-in demonstrations in the past few years.

King, 33, is a Baptist minister and a native of Georgia.

His appearance here will be the first in a College Union series featuring nationally prominent figures.

MARTIN LUTHER KING, JR.

Ruling Made For Students On Probation

A student on probation at the end of the spring semester now has only one summer school

Bernice Davenport shows the historic marker placed at the church. She was the church organist. The songs that day were "The Battle Hymn of the Republic" and "Rock-a-My Soul." (Courtesy of Triad Cultural Arts.)

CULTURAL AND HISTORIC MARKERS

(Former) Atkins High School, located at 1215 North Cameron Avenue

African-American West End, located at BB&T Ballpark

Bethania Freedmen's Community, located at Bethania-Rural Hall Road

Carver High School, located at 3545 Carver School Road

Colored Baptist Orphanage Home opened in 1905, located in the Belview Community

Depot Street Graded School, located at 7th Street and Patterson Avenue

First Sit-In Victory in North Carolina, located on 4th Street near Liberty Street intersection

George Black House and Brick Yard, located at 111 Dellabrook Road

Happy Hill Neighborhood, located at Alder Street

Kate Bitting Reynolds Memorial Hospital, located at North Cleveland Avenue and East Seventh Street

Lloyd Presbyterian Church established in the 1870s, located at 748 Chestnut Street

Oak Grove School built in 1910, located at 2637 Oak Grove Circle

Odd Fellows Cemetery, located at 2881 Shorefair Drive

Safe Bus Company, located at 100 West Fifth Street

Simon G. Atkins, located on US 311 (Martin Luther King Jr. Drive) at Cromartie Street

Simon Green Atkins House, located on the Campus of Winston-Salem State University

The Pond Neighborhood, located at Northwest Boulevard and North Trade Street

Winston Salem State University, located on US 311 (Martin Luther King Jr. Drive) at Cromartie Street

Winston-Salem Chapter of the Black Panther Party, located at North Martin Luther King Jr. Drive & East Fifth Street

BIBLIOGRAPHY

Across the Creek from Salem: The Story of Happy Hill, 1816–1952. The Gallery at Old Salem, February 7 to June 7, 1998. Exhibition Text, 1998.

Crews, C. Daniel. *Neither Slave nor Free Moravians, Slavery, and a Church That Endures.* Winston Salem, NC: Moravian Archives, 1998.

Rohrer, Scott S. *Freedman of the Lord, The Black Moravian Congregation of Salem, N.C., and its Struggle for Survival, 1856-1890.* 1993.

Oppermann, Langdon E. *Winston-Salem's African-American Neighborhoods: 1870-1950.* Architectural and Planning Report. Winston Salem, NC, 1994.

Korstad, Robert Rodgers. *Civil Rights Unionism, Tobacco Workers and the Struggle for Democracy in the Mid-Twentieth-Century South.* Chapel Hill, NC: University of North Carolina Press, 2003.

Davis, Lenwood G., William J. Rice, and James H. McLaughlin. *African Americans in Winston-Salem/Forsyth County.* Virginia Beach, VA: The Donning Company/Publishers, 1999.

Murphy, E. Louise. *The History of Winston-Salem State University: 1892–1995.* Virginia Beach, VA: The Donning Company/Publishers, 1999.

McMillan, Felecia Piggott. *The North Carolina Black Repertory Company: 25 Marvtastic Years.* Greensboro, NC: Open Hand Publishing, LLC, 2005.

DISCOVER THOUSANDS OF LOCAL HISTORY BOOKS
FEATURING MILLIONS OF VINTAGE IMAGES

Arcadia Publishing, the leading local history publisher in the United States, is committed to making history accessible and meaningful through publishing books that celebrate and preserve the heritage of America's people and places.

Find more books like this at
www.arcadiapublishing.com

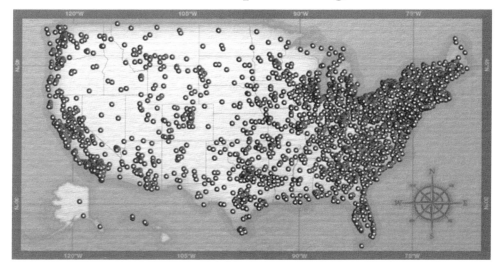

Search for your hometown history, your old stomping grounds, and even your favorite sports team.

Consistent with our mission to preserve history on a local level, this book was printed in South Carolina on American-made paper and manufactured entirely in the United States. Products carrying the accredited Forest Stewardship Council (FSC) label are printed on 100 percent FSC-certified paper.

MADE IN THE USA